LIVE BRIEFS

LIVE BRIEFS

A political sketch book

Steve Bell and Simon Hoggart

Methuen

Dedicated to our families

First published in Great Britain in 1996
by Methuen London
an imprint of Reed International Books Ltd
Michelin House, 81 Fulham Road, London SW3 6RB
and Auckland, Melbourne, Singapore and Toronto

The cartoons first published in the *Guardian* in 1989, 1990, 1994, 1995, 1996. The cartoons on pages 101, 140, 165, 166, 167, 168, 169 first published in the *New Statesman* in 1987, 1988, 1989, 1990. All other sketches previously unpublished

Designed by Brian Homer
Production by Brian Homer and Trevor Carter
Edited by Steve Bell and Brian Homer

A CIP catalogue record for this book
is available at the British Library
ISBN 0 413 70970 1

Printed and bound in Great Britain
by Clays Ltd, St Ives plc

CONTENTS

IMPORTANT PANTS NOTE

People often ask why Steve Bell always draws the Prime Minister with his trademark underpants outside his trousers – the celebrated Pants of Power. Steve's original idea was to make him look like Superman, only with sturdy, humdrum Marks & Spencer Y-fronts instead of the glamorous thingies which the Man of Steel favours. Contrary to received wisdom, this has nothing to do with the later discovery – made when he bent over during a press briefing at the back of his plane – that he likes to tuck his shirt-tails into his underpants.

INTRODUCTION:
Notes from the Margin

You hold in your hand a rare phenomenon, a book that is exactly what it says it is on the cover. This is a political sketch book. Simon Hoggart writes sketches, I draw them. When I first approached Simon with the idea of doing a book together it was because I thought I needed text to illustrate my free-standing cartoons, and Simon agreed because I have a feeling he needed drawings to illustrate his writings.

As it turned out we both ended up illustrating our own points of view, Simon as a Westminster insider, me as a Brighton based outsider. Neither of us go into the Farringdon Road offices of the *Guardian* very much, though we both share that paper's ideal of a Quest for Gags informed by a Lust for Truth. We also both very much appreciate its hands-off, laissez-faire style of editorial intervention in our work, as well as the money it regularly pays us.

Steve Bell
August 1996

A little while ago I was in a bookshop. A man peered at me. 'Are you that bloke in the *Guardian*?' he asked. 'I really like the way you stick it to those politicians,' he went on. 'Coz you see I hate them, all of the bastards, I really loathe every stinking one of them, God, they make me sick, that's why I like what you write – you hate those miserable bastards every bit as much as me…'

As I fled the shop, I knew that I could never live up to my new friend's exacting standards. But Steve Bell does.

Simon Hoggart
August 1996

JOHN MAJOR:
Mission Incomprehensible

LOST IN EUROSPACE

Who could have guessed that those well-loved old proverbs would sink so deep into the young boy's mind and emerge decades later, when he had – astonishingly – become Prime Minister of the very country which had funded his learning?

I have long held the theory that John Major learned to speak English in Nigeria. It accounts for so much. The mysterious lacunae in his life story. The family's unexplained change of name from Major-Ball to Major. Most convincing of all are his curious vocabulary and speech patterns.

My belief is that, rather than merely having worked as a banker in Nigeria, he was born there. As a barefoot boy with a thirst for knowledge he would run across the bush, through the desert and the jungle, on his way to the nearest British Council library. Here he would find, reproduced in the tropics, a reading room from a small south-coast town in England similar in almost every detail, except for the fan slicing slowly through the soupy air.

On the shelves he would find, alongside Shakespeare and Dickens, shelves of books by Agatha Christie, Dorothy L. Sayers and – if the librarian had an eye for the daringly modern novel – Ngaio Marsh and Margery Allingham. There would be yellowing back copies of the bound weekly edition of the *Daily Mirror* filled with ads

9

hinting at impossible wealth: the new Ford 'Consul', only £525.

But our bright-eyed young student does not pause there for long. Instead he makes straight for the shelf marked 'English language'. Here, with dust-stained fingers, he takes down a book entitled *Speak English the Way the English Do*, curls up in a wickerwork chair, and loses himself in the magical resonances of the world's most widely spoken tongue.

'English people have many colourful phrases which give life and vigour to their discourse. All of these will be understood by your English interlocutor, and none will give offence. When you want to tell an English person that you think his comments may have gone a little too far, and that it is not his part to say what he has just said, say to him, "It's a bit rich!"... If you wish to tell an English friend that actions speak louder than words, declare, "Fine words butter no parsnips!"'

The boy reads on. Outside, the velvet tropical night falls swiftly, and the librarian tells him that she is locking up for the night. He begs to borrow the book, and with a kindly twinkle she agrees. Later that night, under a guttering paraffin lamp, he reads on until sleep can be held at bay no longer.

Who could have guessed that those well-loved old proverbs would sink so deep into the young boy's mind and emerge decades later, when he had – astonishingly – become Prime Minister of the very country which had funded his learning? It is a remarkable tribute to the British Council (which over the years has achieved an extraordinary amount for Britain's interests abroad and so naturally

is having its grant cut) that this humble Nigerian library should have had such an effect on the history of our nation. And if anyone points out that for someone of African descent John Major is the wrong colour, I say, look at Michael Jackson.

Most of the successful Majorisms give the impression that they have been learned from books rather than from conversation. When he says, 'Labour and taxes go together like strawberries and cream!' you find yourself thinking vaguely, aren't strawberries and cream supposed to be nice? Shouldn't he have said 'like Burke and Hare', or 'like vomiting and diarrhoea'? But you know what has happened; he has read somewhere that 'when English people want to say that two things always come together, they say they are "like strawberries and cream".' Because demotic language can only be learned through usage and not through books, it sounds wrong, like the apocryphal East European: 'You think I know fuck nothing. In fact, I know fuck all!'

The whiff of the past kept creeping into the speech he made to the 1995 Conservative Party conference. Rhetoric is supposed to pull the listener headlong towards the speaker's destination. But Major's oratory has the opposite effect. It puts up fences and digs ditches to slow you down. Instead of the jokes adding the effervescent excitement, they make you stop listening for a while as you puzzle out exactly what he meant.

'Labour say they know how to run a market economy. I asked Humphrey the Cat about that! I've never seen him run so fast!' The loyal audience laughed the driest and most nervous of laughs. What

MAJOR — "RELAXED ON FISH" — OFFICIAL

·706·21·12·95~   ~©SteveBell 1995~

has the Downing Street cat got to do with running a market economy? If Major had said, 'Labour claim they are going to double VAT on pet food – I've never seen Humphrey run so fast!' you could begin to understand it. And why should the cat be afraid of Labour's boasts about the market economy? Again, if he had said, 'Labour claim they are going to repeal the Dangerous Dogs Act,' one could have understood the humorous point behind Humphrey's imagined panic.

Moments later he introduced us to another domestic animal. This was beginning to resemble *Pets Win Prizes* but without Dale Winton's macho style. 'The Liberals are the only Party in British political history that has had its entire battle plans wiped clean off the media – by a goldfish. My goldfish!'

The speech moved onward, but our minds were stuck behind, like a rambler's trousers snagged on barbed wire. His goldfish? Ah yes, he had announced earlier that summer that a golfish in his pond at home in Huntingdon had been suffering from the heat. So he had rubbed suntan oil into the tiny creature's sore back. This important event had received more attention in the newspapers of the day than the launch of a new Liberal Democrat manifesto, hence the jibe. Yet instead of listening to the speech, we were left behind pondering this evocative image of

12

our Prime Minister rubbing Factor 15 into a fish.

He went on. For some reason he discerned an arcane significance in the fact that George Orwell's real name was Blair. (Mr Major seems mildly obsessed by Orwell. His famous description of England as a land of 'warm beer, cricket pitches and old maids cycling to communion' was lifted more or less whole from Orwell, though we are now a land of empty churches, chilled lager, and school cricket pitches which have been flogged off by the council to keep the tax bills down.)

'He [Orwell] changed his name! I can't say the same thing about the Leader of the Opposition. He's changed everything else!' (I suppose if, like Major, you have changed your name, you might well regard it as a sign of trustworthiness.)

Nothing would stop him. Suddenly we were in a boys' comic and a strip cartoon, possibly about a heroic young lad in the Crusades: 'Choice is liberty! Blazon it on your mind!' Then we were back in the British Council reading room in Kano, Nigeria. 'If we had followed Labour's advice, we'd have been on Carey Street years ago.' When did you last hear someone say that? But it must be there somewhere in *English for Foreigners Made Easy* (1929): 'If you hear that someone is in danger of being declared bankrupt, you can say that they are "in danger of going to Carey Street".'

He tried some more jokes. They landed leadenly on the delegates like cow-pats in a meadow. He mentioned Fettes School in Scotland. Tony Blair attended Fettes, a fact well known to those of us who follow politics, and so almost entirely unknown to delegates at the Conservative Party conference. 'Quite a lot of famous politicians went to Fettes – including [long pause] Iain Macleod!' Probably many of the delegates hadn't heard of Iain Macleod either. Why were they being told this? If they did understand the reference, what could it mean? That Fettes School has a reputation for educating the very finest politicians? Or some of the worst? Whole passionate paragraphs of oratory flow past while the brain frets about such conundrums, like a piece of bacon lodged between the teeth.

Then followed an intriguing passage. Someone had obviously told him that his greatest asset was his sincerity. If only the public could see the real John Major, the decent, honest, open, unpretentious fellow who lives behind the peevish, scheming politician, they would instinctively respond to him and say, in spite of everything, he's really just like us. In fact, what they say is, what a dork.

Take this passage from the speech about his father:

'When I was a small boy my bread and butter was paid for by my father's small business. He made garden ornaments forty years ago,

and some fashionable people find that very funny. I don't.'

But they do? I know very few fashionable people myself, but I've met one or two, here and there, and I can honestly say that not one has sniggered at the subject of the Prime Minister's father's trade. ('Garden ornaments' has a nice, Majorish ring to it, meaning, basically, gnomes. I once knew a woman whose husband was a bookie's runner. She always said that he was 'an accountant to a turf accountant'.) He went on:

'I see the proud, stubborn, independent old man who ran that firm, and taught me to love my country, fight for my own, and spit in the eye of malign fate. I know the knockers and sneerers who may never have taken a risk in their comfortable lives aren't fit to wipe the boots of the risk takers of Britain.'

That passage was meant to have the conference roaring its approval. True Tories are the real backbone of Britain, as true Tories never tire of telling you. Yet it didn't get the required result. They clapped courteously, but without enthusiasm, and no wonder, because the passage – meant to bring us the distilled quintessence of Major – was a clunker. The metaphors weren't so much mixed as whizzed up in a Cuisinart. For instance, 'spit in the eye of malign fate' is an example of an undead metaphor, brought back to life by a mistaken juxtaposition. ('Flogging a dead horse' is fine; 'Flogging a dead horse brought down at the Beecher's Brook of Labour's policy on competition' is gruesome. We have an instant mental image of Malign Fate paying a visit to Major Senior's gnomeyard, and the old man spitting at him, rudely.

AFTER GAINSBOROUGH - ©Steve Bell 1995 - 556·31·1·95

Then he creates an army of straw men to knock down. These are the people who laughed at his father, not only for making gnomes, which, let's face it, now he comes to mention it, is quite funny, but for failing in business. That failure makes him one of the Risk Takers of Britain, presumably from a long, proud tradition which includes King Alfred and Sir Francis Drake. And why do they have dirty boots? Did he mean 'lick the boots of the risk takers of Britain'? But that implies cringing servility. And while we're at it, what's so shameful about being a shoeshine boy? Many of our finest risk takers started out earning money in such humble occupations.

A Major speech ought to be an exhilarating hike. But you never reach the end, because you're constantly pulled up by little puzzles. It has a surrealist, dreamlike quality. How did an old supermarket trolley get on top of that steeple? Why is there a giraffe in that field of sheep?

The effect of these weirdnesses is all the greater because an important set speech has been prepared over many days by many people. You would expect extempore answers, often delivered in the heat of Prime Minister's Question Time in the Commons, to be odder still. And so they are, but in a different way. Here Mr Major's vocabulary tends to become separated from his synapses. The effect is a little like watching the spell-check on a computer; there is a slight but disoncerting lapse between the word being uttered and the brain confirming that it is the right choice.

Take his remark in June 1995 during Question Time. We couldn't know that hot afternoon that he had made up his mind to resign the

16

Tory leadership and run for re-election. His mind must have been engaged on more pressing matters, which is why, called upon to deliver a ringing denunciation of terrorism, he said, 'Terrorism is unpleasant, and should be resisted!'

Sometimes, as with Greece and Turkey, one senses that he and the English language have grudgingly decided to live together, but have never quite made their peace:

'The Opposition likes to take credit for the information superhigway. But if they were to take their heads out of the sand and put their heads into holes in the road, they would see that it is already being built!'

Now and again we are back in the playground, taunting our school friends and, as with children, a certain amount of logic-chopping is necessary here. Tony Blair was attacking him over rail privatisation, and he responded by pointing out that Labour had failed to condemn a series of strikes on the railways. The argy-bargy went back and forth for a few minutes without result, then Major eventually felt he had capped it all by declaring, 'All I can say is, it's a good job I'm not going to Australia by train!'

Mr Blair does seem, like BSE, to have a spongifying effect on his brain. At one recent Question Time the Opposition leader accused Mr Major of having moved his Party to the right. This was the reply:

'The centre right is our ground, and there is no way a squatter like yourself will be able to rest on it. You may regard yourself as the Trojan Horse of socialism, but you will find that it's our land you are parking on.'

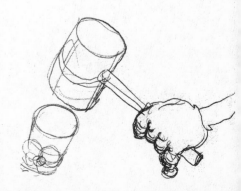

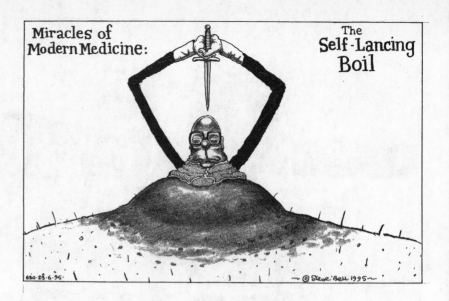

Again, the surrealist dream–vision: a vast Trojan Horse parked on a patch of waste ground, a yellow clamp fixed to its leg.

Horses, goldfish, cats – animals generally seem to have a paralysing effect on his speech. So does Paddy Ashdown, whose interventions (generally delivered in a high moral tone) seem to drive Mr Major to a gibbering fury. When livestock and the Liberal leader are combined, the effect can be cataclysmic. Mr Ashdown had implied that the Prime Minister had said different things to the British people than he had to other heads of government at an EU meeting.

Mr Ashdown, he replied, had been 'talking complete, unadulterated rubbish, and went on doing so for some time'. Mr Ashdown shook his head at this. Mr Major began to froth: 'Oh, he was there was he? It was he who brought in the tea, and the coffee, and the biscuits!… He doesn't even know the effect of a partial emu!'

One imagines that the partial emu is some wretched flightless bird, sliced in half, suspended in formaldehyde by Damien Hirst.

Things do not improve when real animals are the topic. One festive season Mr Tony Banks, the Commons' leading enthusiast for animal rights, asked him to ask people not to ask for puppies at Christmas. He referred to the nine-word slogan, 'A puppy is for life, not just for Christmas.' But this was too crisp, too short-winded for the Prime Minister. He recast it in thirty-one words: 'I hope that everyone bears in mind that it is a present for the long term and not just the short term and I hope everyone will bear that in mind.' (To Mr Major, 'To be or not to be' would be re-translated in his head to: 'It is important that we take this opportunity to contemplate an on-going existence scenario…')

One of his more alarming techniques is to take a perfectly ordinary political barb, and imply that it is a disgrace to the Mother of Parliaments. He treats normal tub-thumping as if it were an assualt on Mother Teresa. (He has, oddly, used the word 'motherhood' to condemn an intervention he thought merely a truism – presumably short for 'motherhood and apple pie'.) I've

made this one up, but it is typical:

Labour MP: 'Will the Prime Minister not admit it is appalling that the crime rate has risen by forty-seven per cent in the last two years alone, and that sending yet more people to prison is not the answer?'

Major (quietly, as if restraining himself with difficulty): 'I think the Honourable Member may, in time, regret the manner in which he asked that question.'

Here's a real example. A Labour MP asked him whether he might not ponder Gandhi's dictum, 'There is enough in the world for everyone's need, but not enough for everyone's greed.' This struck some of us as a graceful way of making the point, but Mr Major was horrified. You would have thought that quoting Gandhi was the most cyncial piece of mischief-making since Iago first whispered in Othello's ear. He said grimly, 'I think everyone who heard that intervention, and the millions who may have watched it on television, will form their own judgement of its value!'

In fact, only a few thousand would have seen it live on television, and I doubt if it was repeated on any news programme. But Major seemed to believe that the exchange would inflame public opinion across the kingdom.

There is a pub which exists only in the Conservative imagination. Michael Heseltine has been known to refer to it as the Dog and Duck. As they drink their warm beer, the regulars at the Dog and Duck epitomise good, honest, British forbearance and fair play – coupled, of course, with their rugged determination not to see

19

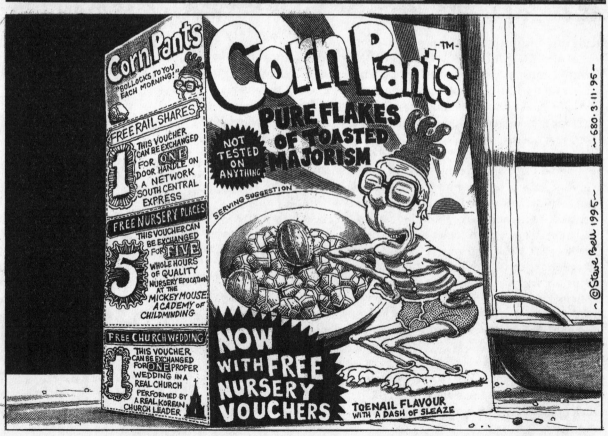

Britain sold short. These drinkers are characterised as much by what they don't discuss as by what they do. 'I doubt they'll be talking about that in the Dog and Duck tonight,' a Minister will say about some example of socialistic nit-picking.

It's a schizophrenic kind of place, the old Dog and Duck. A pro-European Minister will announce, drawing on his deep reservoir of sympathetic feeling with the British people, 'I wonder just how many people in the Dog and Duck are going to be debating the single European currency tonight!' while his sceptical colleague will say that, more and more, in pubs and clubs up and down the land, people are beginning to realise that a single European currency would be fatally damaing to our prospects.

Clearly Mr Major was expecting that conversation in the snug would be along these lines:

Ted: 'Thanks, I will have another, Dennis, since you twist my arm. Now, I don't mind saying, I had been thinking on voting Labour this time out. But, by heck, when that feller stood up in Parliament and started quoting Gandhi – what was it, enough for everyone's need but not for their greed, or some other such Communist claptrap, I don't know what – I thought, stuff it, I'll stick wi' Tories, when all's said.'

Bill: 'No, no, you've got it arse over tip, Ted. It were worse than that. It wasn't quoting that little brown bugger that got our Prime Minister riled. It were that fellow implying that John Major hisself weren't concerned wi' poor and disadvantaged in our society. That's what got him going, and I for one don't blame 'im…

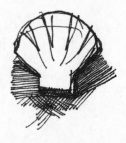

MAJORLAND
A Grammar School in every town
A Prison in every living room
A Cow in every fireplace

© Steve Bell 1996 1757 5-4-96

President George Bush had his 'Bushisms', in which a train of thought disappeared down a thousand branch lines. But Mr Major has no connected train; rather he has a single runaway caboose, hurtling wherever the points decree. When it comes to using the language, no one could accuse Mr Major of not being one of the Risk Takers of Britain:

'When your back's against the wall, you've got to turn round and march forward!'

Or straight back into the wall, if you think about it. There was the junior Labour spokesman who tackled him on some report or other which was critical of the government. Major taunted him: 'I see from looking at your face that all you have read is the Press Association extract!'

And my personal favourite, which expresses guts and stubbornness in true Majorish fashion. Here he is in 1995 immediately after winning back the leadership he had resigned. He stood solemnly in front of the cameras and microphones and declared to the waiting nation, 'I shall now return to Downing Street!'

The wonderful thing was, he was standing in Downing Street at the time.

LET'S DO CONFERENCE!

Now the conferences are devised to be on television. They have the cosy blandness of Good Morning with Anne and Nick…

Party conferences, particularly those on the Left, used to be vicious, violent affairs. People literally got beaten up for holding the wrong opinions. The toilet in the Imperial Hotel, Blackpool, was especially dangerous.

But those days are gone. Now the conferences are devised to be on television. They have the cosy blandness of *Good Morning with Anne and Nick*. You half expect the chairman to say, 'Well, what a great debate on social security that was! But now, it's time once again for Carlos, our kooky cook, with some tips on getting the best out of broccoli…' This has had the opposite effect from the one intended. Since few people on the platform ever say anything untoward, or even interesting, the TV coverage concentrates on interviews which are conducted on the sidelines while the conference continues, untelevised, in the hall.

Quite often the TV presenters can engineer a disagreement (or 'split shock' in the patois of the trade) by conducting rival discussions. 'So you're telling us, Mr Smith, that you would never contemplate capital punishment in Britain's schools. But just a

moment ago Mr Jones told us it was "very much an option".'

Nowhere is the new blandness more obvious than at the TUC conference, the annual gathering of what used to be termed the 'union barons'. The difference between now and a quarter-century ago is that the conferees seem at ease in suits. They probably wear them all the time. They look not like horny-handed sons of toil, still less like the vanguard of the proletarian revolution, more like a Rotary Club after a good lunch. Even the conference slogan is reassuring: 'Your Voice at Work'. One imagines the banner held up at the head of a march: above the slogan is a lovingly stitched version of those annoying corporate pictures of a smiling young woman on the phone, or an impossibly nice young man beaming at his welding equipment.

Every now and again you may spot a trade union leader who has actually held a strike. Mr Jimmy Knapp, for instance, whose union has caused inconvenience to at least tens of London commuters. But the likes of him are rare. The tone is more appropriately caught by the conference programme, which is packed with glossy ads for public relations firms and vouchers for free *sake* in Japanese restaurants. It would look at home in an airline seat pocket.

Throughout the first day of the conference the only fiery, red-blooded speech came, oddly enough, from Mr Gordon Taylor of the Professional Footballers' Association. He declared that the minimum wage ought to be pegged to that of Alan Shearer (Newcastle and England), a position which even Arthur Scargill might hesitate to take. Mr Taylor demanded an end to discrimination in football, on

grounds of 'colour, creed, religion, race or sex'. The first four we can
all agree with; the last seems symptomatic of the TUC's new
obsession with modernisation. In the old days, they would have
been outraged at the prospect of woman football players taking the
wages from male breadwinners; ten years ago they would have
passed a resolution demanding a minimum of four women in every
Premiership team. Now perhaps they will set up a working party
which, in two years, will produce a glossy book entitled *Woman On –
Exploring the Role of Gender in Football 2000*.

Meanwhile, the grand old names of the seventies and eighties,
from the era when British strikes were the envy of the world –
Natsopa, NUPE, the NUR – have mostly vanished, replaced by
strange acronyms, the result of multitudinous mergers, many of
which bring to mind more than the trade they represent. Some are
obvious: NUDAGO (domestic appliance makers) clearly speaks for
Spanish sunbathers. NUMAST (merchant seamen) is the miracle
alloy banned from the America's Cup. UNISON (health workers)
are really a sexual advice clinic, slogan: 'Hoping you will come
together'. NUKFAT (clothing workers) was the code-name for the
atomic bomb the Japanese were working on just before Hiroshima.

How have the Rossendale boot, shoe and slipper makers
managed to stay independent, when their name, RUBSSO, suggests
the most ruthless of all Russian mafia gangs? GUALO (weavers) are
a left-wing terrorist group in a hitherto unknown Central American
state. SUPLO (Scottish power loom overseers) is a comforting
bandage for arthritis sufferers.

MOMINT (military musical instrument makers) is what your Swedish au pair says when you ask her to get off the phone. MSF is the initials of the new medical condition which afflicts people who spend too much time on the Internet. NACODS (colliery overseers) ought to be the union for Scottish eunuchs.

The mood of obsessive reasonableness continued on the second day of the conference, which was addressed by Tony Blair. He was greeted by a courteous demonstration concerning the minimum wage: 'Hey, hey, Tony Blair, £4 for an hour is only fair!' The only way they could have been more moderate would be to change their chant to something even more reasonable: 'Hey, hey, Tony Blair, a minimum wage sensibly and flexibly introduced in the light of prevailing economic circumstances, should not cause anyone to lose their hair.'

Mr Blair's speech was, as ever, extremely cunning. He has a knack of carrying people along with his rhetoric, and it is only after he has finished that they begin to worry about what he has actually said. This is how he pushed the abolition of Clause 4 past a bemused Labour conference in 1994. This time he was the married man taking his mistress out for what he knows, and she doesn't, is their last dinner together. It was only after the dessert and the armagnac that he told them he wouldn't be seeing quite so much of them in future. 'It's not distance I want, but clarity,' he told the union leaders. 'The nature of our relationship will of course change over time…'

If the TUC had been paying attention, it is at this point that it

would have thrown the glass of wine into his face and marched out of the restaurant. But like all the great seducers, Mr Blair knows that there is as much skill in ending an affair quietly as there is to getting the girl into bed in the first place.

The Liberals hold the first political assembly of the year, and a thunderous anti-climax it usually is. It is the one conference where, to pass the time, you find yourself reading the programme. In Glasgow this included a glossary of the local dialect, so that delegates would understand what was said to them in the streets outside. These included colourful phrases such as 'Awa, and raffle yer doughnut' (please leave), and 'Ah haveny got a scooby' (I do not have a scooby).

Some notion of the normal course of political debate in Scotland could be gathered from the police, who patrolled the gigantic and dreary conference hall – possibly a hangar used for repainting 747s when there's no conference in town – equipped with handcuffs and riot batons, as if afraid that the debate on a non-polluting transport policy might turn nasty. ('The accused was shouting aggressively about the need for a multi-modal pan-European strategy. After I had clearly instructed him to raffle his doughnut, I slapped the cuffs on…')

What is disconcerting about these assemblies for an old cynic like me is that these people are interested in policy rather than shafting each other. They not only defend your right to have heretical opinions; they will applaud you for holding them. On the

first day of the assembly, one man spoke in favour of dumping disused oil platforms on the ocean bed. This view, roughly on a par with suggesting that the French should be allowed to use Twyford Down for nuclear tests, received courteous if distant applause, a little like the sound of seaweed flapping in a rock pool.

Labour motions tend to be yearning, unattainable aspirations. Tory motions are sickly sweet with compliments, the verbal equivalent of golden syrup poured all over Tory Ministers. But Liberal motions are vastly detailed, covering every aspect of the subject, considering every eventuality. Some cover several pages of clauses, sub-clauses, and sub-paragraphs and are debated line by line. Scarcely a conjunction or preposition lacks its passionate defenders. The 'chair' will describe how the balloting is to take place: 'We are now going to vote on "and" or "or". You may not vote for "and" and "or", only for either "or" or "and"…'

In Glasgow Helen Bailey declared bravely from the platform, 'I want to take the votes on the separate votes before the votes on the amendments.' What is most amazing is that everyone present knew exactly what she was talking about. Later someone else said, 'There will be a separate vote on the word "rapid" and then a separate vote on from the words "to the end" to the end.' At this point someone at the back of the hall laughed a short yet maniacal laugh, as if a tortured spirit had finally broken free.

Liberals love high-tech. Their schtick is that the two main parties are mired in traditional ways of thought, while they – their

28

imaginations untrammelled – soar on the jetstream of innovation. Lord Beaumont declared, 'Fellow Liberals, we live in a world in which Danish pastries are flown from Copenhagen to New York, and Danish pastries are flown from New York to Copenhagen. And the planes pass each other on the way.' (That's lucky, one thought; otherwise the people of Greenland would be knee-deep in flaky pastry and jam.)

His solution was, of course, the Internet, which people could use to swap recipes. But what other Party would even perceive, still less discuss, the Danish pastry problem?

They also love jargon. In the debate on world trade, they discussed approvingly the 'presumption of compatibility'. You know instinctively that these are the kind of people who talk about the presumption of compatibility in pubs.

Deep down, whatever they say, they don't want power. In power, issues such as the presumption of compatibility would disappear. Nobody would talk about it. Civil servants would make sure the phrase never appeared on any ministerial paper. Advertising men in silly glasses would counsel, ' "Vote LibDem for presumed compatibility" does nothing at all for me, sweetypie.' Ms Liz Lynne, for example, would be told – if not in so many words – that she shouldn't bother her pretty little head

Labour home page

new Labour Lasting prosperity　Home Economics Page
1: Windfall Tax　2: Release Council receipts　3: er...that's it

a1　　　　a2　　　　aa4

new Labour

new **Britain**

no **piggy backs**

© Steve Bell/The Bellworks 1995

about the presumption of compatibility.

Power would mean compromising principles. Power would mean having to compromise between 'and' and 'or' instead of having a crisp, clear vote on each. It's a harsh thing to say, but the Liberals in power would be like trainspotters running a privatised railway. It's not the point; it's not why they stand day after day on the draughty platform. At bottom, if they were completely honest, they don't want the red meat of power, so much as the Spam sandwiches of the sidings.

Over at the Labour conference, I went to the stand occupied by the Royal College of Midwives. There, alongside pictures of breast-feeding mothers, a Labour MP called Michael Connarty tried on something called the Empathy Belly. First he was fitted with a belt around his chest to provide a sensation of tightness. Then they put on the belly itself, with its large and unwieldly bosom. Into a cavity in the stomach they slotted a plastic bladder, capable of holding a gallon or so. Finally they added two lead weights, in order to create the near impossibility of standing up or getting out of the bath.

So accoutred, Mr Connarty was able to experience for himself something which most men will never comprehend – the sensation of being Roy Hattersley.

No, he didn't! That was a cheap crack. Mr Hattersley is now almost slender. Mr Connarty meanwhile said that he had been suffering from morning sickness, 'but you always get that after two days at the Labour Party conference'. Leaflets at the stall explained how couples could go on having sex until late in pregnancy. Thank goodness he didn't try to demonstrate that; the bladder looked lethal.

30

The stalls at the Labour conference – and there are more than a hundred of them – demonstrate how much the Party has changed. Norman Tebbit was patrolling the fringe, representing BT, which had made a deal with Tony Blair to put free computer uplinks in British schools and hospitals (in exchange for access to cable television entertainment which, since the schools will have to pay BT for the use of the phone lines, makes it one of the better business deals since the Indians traded Manhattan). I was approached by an affable fellow from the Country Landowners' Association. Whatever next? The Confederation of Beer-Waterers? PROs explaining over drinks that silk-hatted financiers are people too? Cedric Brown?

Labour has become obsessed with the Internet too, even though many of the people who use it are the kind who, if they talked to you in a railway carriage, would cause you to pull the communication cord and leap for freedom. Mr Chris Smith raved that the whole nation would be linked up, so we could 'report a pothole! Or call up a page from Hansard!' One woman combined two icons of New Labour by declaring that, thanks to the Internet, 'Tony Blair has told us that faults in an oil rig in the Gulf of Mexico can be diagnosed in Aberdeen!' with the implication that it must be true because Tony Blair said it. One sometimes heretically ponders, why couldn't the Mexican oil rigger just get on the phone?

The main evening task for Party conference goers is gatecrashing. This can be just difficult enough to make it an amusing sport. Most, however, are easy. The people who have organised the party know their superiors will judge them by how many people turn up. So even if you weren't invited, you enhance their prestige by your presence. Anything with 'Europe' in the title is going to be easy to get in to (for some reason, the more exotic the name of the organisation, the more likely they are to provide mediocre wine supplied by the hotel). You simply march in, wave graciously at the young ladies on the desk at the door, and sweep towards the drinks tray as if it were you who were bestowing your favour upon them.

Some are impossible. Short of producing an AK-47, you are unlikely ever to crash the Saatchi and Saatchi party at the Tory conference. BA is tricky too. A group of us once effected an entrance by claiming that Lord King's son-in-law was a close colleague. There was a moment of pure anguish for the chap in the purser's uniform on the door. He knew that there was only a one-per-cent chance that this was true – yet, he must have asked himself, was that worth a one-per-cent chance of risking his job? He glowered angrily, and we had the grace to look shamefaced as we shuffled in, though as it happened our claim was perfectly true. It's not lying, but being thought by others to be lying, which creates embarrassment.

The simplest way of getting into the mid-range parties is to turn up, glance around the room from the door, wave heartily at someone you know – or possibly someone

you've never seen in your life – and march in, as if your eagerness to be with them prevents you from even remembering the courtesy of a check-in. Since few of the young ladies are going to pursue you into the middle of the room, you're almost certainly safe. If by some horrible chance you are challenged, appear apologetic: 'I'm so sorry, how rude of me. I'm here with the conference arrangements people, and we were asked if we'd like to send someone along. It's little old me, I'm afraid…' Remember, the people who are running the party aren't paying for it. Deep down, they do not care.

Revels continue through the night. The Brighton bomb of 1984 would have killed far more people if it hadn't been timed for 3.00 a.m., long before many delegates are even thinking of their beds. Willie Whitelaw once famously retired late and told his wife that he had been unable to get away from the relentless questioning of the journalists in the bar. This worked until Mrs Whitelaw took the lift down to breakfast in the company of hacks. 'My God, what a night,' said one, not recognising her. 'Willie Whitelaw was in the bar; he wouldn't stop talking, and of course I couldn't go to bed in case he said something really important.' Broadcasts from the conference are now fashionably staged in the hotel lobbies; if you are hanging round at 4.00, there's every chance you'll be able to give your views on Radio Five Live, fascinating at least seven long-distance lorry drivers.

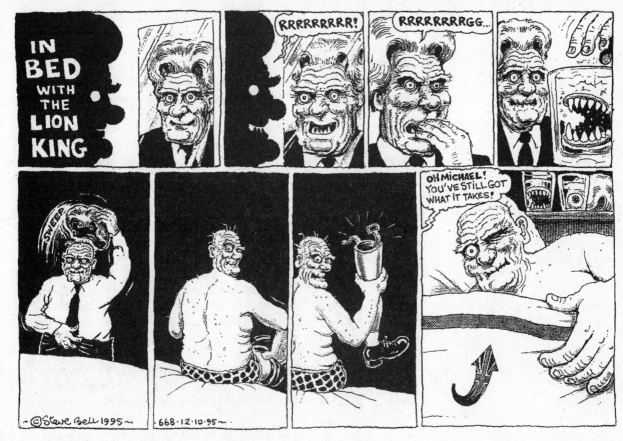

In the hall, the Tory conference is now so smooth, so predictable, so limp and lacklustre, that they have tried to pep it up with set-piece interviews, styled on those American shows which explore grotesque sex lives, such as 'Men who have sex with goats and the women who love them.'

In Blackpool, they looked at an equally bizarre perversion: 'Young people who support the Conservative Party and are not afraid to say so.' The athlete and MP Sebastian Coe descended into the Conference to talk to these pitiful persons. They did not turn out to be a precise cross-section of Generation X.

'What brings you to the conference?' he inquired. 'I'm here because of the opportunities only a Conservative government can provide,' said the young person.

'Well, Ashley, what do you do?' asked Seb, the Robin Day of the nineties. 'I'm a solicitor in Bristol,' said Ashley, 'and I give free legal advice to anyone who wants it!'

'Triffic!' said Seb.

33

A plump young man was the next subject of his merciless grilling. 'Under the Conservatives I can choose whatever school I want to go to. They have raised employment and cut down on crime,' he asserted with blithe disregard for the facts.

'By day I have an excellent job in personnel,' Seb managed to squeeze out of another young humanoid. One yearned for him to add, 'And at night I earn valuable extra cash as a rent boy.' But he did charity work instead. As did Jason. 'Jason, tell us your story,' demanded the relentless inquisitor. He managed somehow to winkle out the fact that Jason divided his time between a demanding university course and charity work.

There were many worst speeches of the conference – Mr Portillo's rant (q.v.) being one. But the most egregiously creepy perhaps came from the Party Chairman, Brian Mawhinney. It's not altogether his fault. Ulster accents can sound honest and open, or they can be wheedling and ingratiating. Why is John Cole one of the most popular broadcasters in Britain and Gerry Anderson driven from Radio 4? Mr Mawhinney belongs among the group who give you goose-pimples even when it's not cold.

He declared roundly that the Conservatives would win the next election. Yet this inevitably rings with a hollow clunk when you know that he is fleeing elsewhere from his constituency of Peterborough, a seat which would be perfectly safe if the Tories were in with a chance. He cannot, however, say this. 'Under John Major we are going to fight to win, though not in Peterborough' does not work. Nor does: 'We will win through because Tory values are British values, even if they are not the values of Peterborough!' And his peroration would have been dismal: 'Our message to our opponents is uncompromising. For the sake of our country, get out of our way. Except in Peterborough!'

I Declare This Shithouse Open

Say what you like about Britain, but we still have the naffest ceremonial in the world. The colourful splendour! The immemorial pageantry! It all looks as if it had been copied out of a Ladybird book.

I always enjoy the State Opening of Parliament. Say what you like about Britain, but we still have the naffest ceremonial in the world. The colourful splendour! The immemorial pageantry! It all looks as if it had been copied out of a Ladybird book.

And the State Opening is one of the few times when you can take Parliament seriously. Instead of politicians making dozens of impossible promises, you have the Queen making impossible promises on their behalf.

The whole thing is so grandiose and pompous and out of date that one can only be grateful for it. The idea that the kind of people who have been 'modernising' Britain for the last few decades might one day get their hands on it is too painful to contemplate.

Of course it is silly. It is quite majestically silly. Look down on the Woolsack in the House of Lords, where all the judges sit in their wigs, buttock to buttock, haunch to haunch, trying not to fall off, like so many transvestite tarts in a Parisian police van.

Glance round the galleries, and it's like finding yourself in the pages of *Hello!* magazine. Isn't that Sarah Armstrong-Jones, who is something to do with the Royal Family? Could that be Cherie Blair, under a hat so vast you could shelter a family of lion cubs in its shade? Down to our left was Jeffrey Archer, the celebrated author, chatting to an elderly and balding peer, whose face I did not recognise, but whose conversation one might surmise. 'Fascinating board meeting yesterday, old boy, much better offer than we'd expected, must be mad, of course I can rely on your discretion…'

There is the American ambassador, Admiral Crowe, sitting in the balcony. If he is well behaved, doesn't eat popcorn during the ceremony or put his feet up on the plush velour, he can expect one day to be promoted to the ground floor.

The Marquess of Bath, known as 'the Loins of Longleat', arrived looking like a sixties rock star, possibly Sibilant Lord Sutch. He flapped a limp hand in a 'hey, man' style wave, and rolled his eyes meaningfully. So good to see these ancient traditions still observed. He sat behind a long row of youngish women, some of them strikingly beautiful. One was wearing a white dress which concealed some of her ample and delightful bosom. All of them were in clothes which were over the top, or in the case of the woman in white, under the top. Could he have brought all his celebrated 'wifelets'? Apparently not; these were married to other peers.

Sir Denis Thatcher sat behind the Press, and we could hear his running commentary. 'Decent cove,' he barked when the Papal Nuncio walked in. His wife (Denis Thatcher's, that is, not the Papal Nuncio's) was on the front bench, between Lords Jenkins and Hailsham. She may well have been aware of Lord Jenkins's most

famous hand gesture, where he cups the hand of a plump young peasant girl. Or perhaps she had prior knowledge of his penchant for thin women with titles, revealed in 1996 in a BBC documentary. Either way she talked firmly and exclusively to Lord Hailsham.

Various heralds appeared. It is a measure of the way we British constantly reinvent our history that heralds used to be humble varlets and serfs of complete obscurity, persons whose names never appeared in *Who's Who*. Thanks to our constant progress towards a classless society, they are now Old Etonians of complete obscurity whose names still don't appear in *Who's Who*.

Howard Pursuivant Extraordinary, without any sign of Howard Pursuivant Quite Normal. Maltravers Herald Extraordinary was, the programme informed us, played by John Robinson, Esq., a name which appears to have been coined solely for use in a Brighton hotel. The part of Comptroller of Her Majesty's Household had gone to David Lightbown, now sadly dead, then the most thuggish of all Tory Whips, whose job – now the Spanish Inquisition has been rehabilitated by historians as a group of concerned clerics who offered coffee and biscuits to dissenters – now includes torture, branding and auto-da-fe for Tory rebels.

Then the Lesser Royals arrived, a pitiful bunch, shortly to be cut off from the Civil List, about to find new homes in Knightsbridge's Cardboard City, sleeping in Harrods' doorway even when there isn't a sale on. Princess Margaret arrived last of the lessers, which meant she only had to go twenty minutes between fags. (The Princess is possibly the most relentless smoker in Britain. A friend who has had the mixed experience of dining with her several times reports that she lights up not only between courses, but between mouthfuls.)

Then the Queen arrived with The Artist Formerly Known As Prince Charles. She waited six or seven minutes while the rabble from the Commons crossed over, summoned from their subfusc Chamber by Black Rod. The peers sat in resentful silence, like members of a Pall Mall club invaded by a gang of football supporters. Peers' wives craned their necks, perhaps hoping to get a glance of David Mellor, and join in the chorus which must be whispered behind his back everywhere he goes: 'What on earth can they possibly see in him?'

Prince Charles looked deeply, unfathomably bored. Her Most Excellent Majesty (is there a Slightly Less Excellent Majesty, and was Fergie a Completely Useless Majesty?) was accompanied by the Lady of the Bedchamber and the Woman of the Bedchamber. What neater class distinction could be found than that between those two titles, especially as neither of them has, probably, emptied a bedpan in her life, and can certainly not do hospital corners?

In the long history of Britain's barnacle-encrusted traditions, one of the most ancient – going back decades, which is longer than most Royal ceremonials – is that the Monarch is obliged to read out the most leaden prose the Downing Street civil service can provide. 'NATO's adaptation to a changing security environment… work to ensure the principle of subsidiarity is applied to European legislation…' all from a Queen whose ancestors used to regard subsidiarity as an excuse to top any baron or dissolve any monastery who got in the way of centralised government.

While his mother talked about terrorism, the Prince of Wales rubbed his nose. When she got on to the United Nations, he rubbed his thigh. As she reached the Jobseekers' Allowance (I find it absolutely appalling, as the Prince would say, that the Sovereign should be obliged to mouth these weasly euphemisms) he gazed at the ceiling, as if to say, 'You can't mean me, guv.'

Back in the Commons, the elected representatives have their own peculiar rituals. Two back-benchers are chosen to thank the Queen for her remarks, as if she had written them herself. These occasions are supposed to be light-hearted, but when I saw the Arch-Greaser Gyles Brandreth rise, my heart grew heavy indeed. After-dinner speakers like Mr Brandreth are best accompanied by a glass of Drambuie and a saucer of Elizabeth Shaw mint crisps; listening to them while sober is a little like eating trifle for breakfast.

Mr Brandreth is the master of fake self-deprecation. False modesty is the only kind he knows. 'My wife heard me described on the radio as an expert on the Marriage Act,' he declared to hoots of laughter. 'She nearly fell off her…' Her what? Her chair? Her bed? Her marital aid purchased at an Anne Summers party? Howls of happy glee drowned Mr Brandreth out.

Traditionally, the Leader of the Opposition then makes a speech attacking the Gracious Speech from the Throne, though not the Gracious Personage who delivered it. As a rule he or she begins with an affable compliment or two for the back-benchers who spoke first. Mr Blair broke tradition, and was pleasingly rude about Mr

Brandreth. Whereas, he said, Douglas Hurd had once been described as 'too clever for the Tory Party', that was not a charge that could be levelled against Mr Brandreth. 'He is a winner of the World Monopoly Championships, so there is a seat on a privatised utility waiting for him. He is also the author of a book called *Great Sexual Disasters* – it is remarkable that he wrote it before he came to this House.' Mr Brandreth squirmed with pleasure at all this attention.

However, not all Mr Blair's jokes were quite so effective, and were often met with silence, except for a strangulated bark from some creep sitting behind him, leaving, for the creep, the awful prospect that Mr Blair would not know who had ejaculated the loyal chortle. Perhaps they should intervene in the speech. 'I thank my right honourable friend for giving way, but it does provide me with the opportunity to say what a truly hilarious drollery that was…'

The Prime Minister replied, but his heart was not really in it. On that particular day the unemployment figures had gone up, the pound had gone down, the monarchy was again under threat, and to top it all, Michael Heseltine had been discharged from hospital in perfect health, having been suffering from a kidney stone caused by an excess build-up of urine. Mr Major may well have agreed that the Deputy Prime Minister needs the piss taking out of him more often.

I find it hard to be as upset as perhaps I should be by all this carry-on. In fact I rather like it, and hope we hang on to it. I don't think it's especially harmful, and I don't imagine that the class system would disappear overnight if we replaced it. Nor do I think it leaves us with an exaggerated view of our importance in the world.

If anything, we in Britain have an exaggerated sense of our own decline. The Thatcher government, far from restoring Britain's pride, has made us yet more conscious of our failings. The French, who seem to have done pretty well by hanging on to a sense of their own limitless dignity, would die for such ceremonial. I see no reason why we should destroy it in the careless way we have tossed away our finest city centres and so much of our countryside.

We've been subjected to a pincer movement over the past seventeen years. The institutions which truly have made this country great in the post-imperial world – public service broadcasting, the NHS, the armed services – have been ferociously attacked from the Right, by an ideology which believes nobody can do any useful work unless motivated by money. But in its enfeebled way the Left has tried to do the same. Tony Blair wants to begin 'reforming' the House of Lords by abolishing voting rights for hereditary peers. It sounds reasonable and democratic. There is a good case for it. But let's not imagine that it will make life better for any individual.

It is the manifest injustice of the Lords which has keep it largely impotent, at least since the last War. Peers can hold up a bill for a year at most; even if they disagree completely with the Commons, they are obliged to accept a bill which comes their way twice running. Money bills they cannot even touch.

These are small powers which they use sparingly, but often with surprising good sense. The appalling Criminal Justice Bill, one of the many spatchcocks of legislation which this government has pushed through Parliament, was savaged by the peers – notably Lords Whitelaw and Carr, plus the Lord Chief Justice himself. Other wise amendments from their lordships, for example removing discretion from local authorities over locking up young offenders, were rolled over by the Commons steamroller, all in the name of democracy.

Take away the hereditary peers, with their dottiness, their ear trumpets, their private obsessions such as flying saucers, and their often weird, dislocated view of the world, and you would leave everything in the hands of the Party Whips. Already they control a cowed House of Commons, where an all-powerful executive welcomes on board only those back-benchers who have proved their servility; they would quickly take over a reformed House of Lords. Whips are of only occasional use at present, since the payroll vote is always outnumbered by the distant ancestors of mediaeval barons and the great-grandsons of Birmingham industrialists who had the good sense to pay large sums of money to political parties. The alternative is total rule by party machine.

Would a reformed Lords be more modern? Yup. Would it be fair? In theory. Would it improve anyone's life, or any bill, by so much as one dot or comma? I very much doubt it. And constitutional reform has already helped to wreck two Labour governments.

In the meantime, I would still prefer to have Gold Stick in Waiting, a Gentleman Usher to the Sword of State, and the whole stupid, outdated, 'irrelevant' gallimaufry, than yet another party hack in power.

THEY SHALL NOT RESIGN!

Imagine if there were several people, mostly better paid than you, whose own living depended on pointing out what a rotten job you were doing.

Is it not obscene, immoral and wrong?' asked Mr Nicholas Winterton, MP. What, we pondered, could he be talking about? The situation in Bosnia? Attempts to persuade members of the public to shop their neighbours on secret social security fraud phone lines? The way in which wealthy donors to the Conservative Party always seem to be top of the list when it comes to dishing out the profits from privatisation?

None of these things. It was obscene, immoral and wrong for Mr Winterton to receive only 74p per mile expenses for driving his car to London. Those who have cars with low running costs, he said, were making a huge profit, whereas those like himself 'who need a more comfortable car in which to travel long distances will be subsidising their mileage'.

At £290 for each round trip from Macclesfield in his Range Rover, one might feel that Mr Winterton is doing all right, especially since this is nearly three times the amount of a First Class rail ticket, which he would be given for nothing anyway. But it does illustrate the

MPs' dilemma: in their view, pay is a moral issue. It is essential that we the public are not paid too much, otherwise we will cause inflation, and of course become slothful. It is equally essential that they are paid oodles of cash in order to make sure that our Parliament is able to attract the very highest standard of legislator. In other words, they need the money not for themselves, but on behalf of us all.

It is as if your plumber were to explain that he had doubled his rates overnight, 'in order that you may continue to have the services of the very finest plumber available'.

I write as a supporter of higher pay for MPs. As they never weary of telling us, they could be earning a great deal more in other professions, most notably the law. (Mr Brian Sedgemore suggested that he could be earning up to £250,000 a year as a barrister, which is, of course, an even greater scandal than the low pay received by MPs.) Most MPs work extremely hard. All are plagued by constituents who seem to think it is their job to make their lives perfect in every way.

One Labour MP tells the horrible story of a woman who came to his regular Saturday surgery and whispered to him, asking if she could have a word about her husband. It turned out that it was his pleasure to have anal intercourse with her, followed immediately by oral sex.

'My God, that's disgusting!' the MP said. 'I certainly had better talk to him.'

'Oh, you don't need to ask him to stop,' she said, 'just ask him to

wash it in between…' This is not entirely untypical of the work they have to do.

Then there is the Press. Imagine if there were several people, mostly better paid than you, whose own living depended on pointing out what a rotten job you were doing. Think of a schoolteacher obliged to get through the day with a sketchwriter taking notes and chortling in the classroom, or with a pundit skulking in the playground, someone billed as 'The Man the Pedagogues Dread'.

That said, there was something faintly nauseating about the last debate on MPs' pay, something liable to cause what Russell Harty would have called a 'mini-retchette'. Mr Tim Sainsbury declared that, as a member of the Remunerations Committee for the family firm, he knew how vital it was to retain men and women of the highest calibre. (Is that why the check-out girls at Sainsbury's are paid such fabulous riches?) He wanted the maximum amount, pronto – though we should not get hold of the idea that this was for themselves. The pay rise was entirely for the benefit of generations yet unborn.

'It is in the interests of future parliaments and future governments that we should accept the recommendations in their entirety, straight away!' he boldly declared, and few of those who sat around him said him nay.

Nobody, but nobody, said they wanted the money to spend on fine wine, elegant clothes, holidays and women. They were all, without exception, speaking for their descendants. Sir Terence

Higgins felt that without the moolah, the quality of government would suffer. 'We need a reserve of MPs who can become Ministers,' he said. From the Labour benches, Mr Alf Morris averred, 'Many of us will be voting not for ourselves, but for our dependents.'

Given that they were voting for history rather than for their own wallets, it is not surprising that they selflessly awarded themselves the maximum possible pay rise.

Yet some months earlier they had, to be fair, voted to reveal how much they were paid by their various outside interests, a recommendation made by the Nolan Committee. (This government defeat was deeply galling, not to the government, but the Labour Party, which had hoped to mount a Great Sleaze Chase lasting several months. They were faced with a rare example of the fox shooting itself.)

Normally MPs are somewhat coy about the precise sums they are paid. Mr David Mellor, for example, whose interests as a 'consultant' are thought to bring him in between £300,000 and one million pounds a year, declined to say how much he was paid by each firm on the grounds that he was paid, not as an MP, but because of his own unique skills. It will be fascinating to see how much more they give him when he has ceased to be an MP, and so has more time to deploy those magical skills on their behalf.

The debate which preceded the vote had its own fascination. The division was to be held on a 'free' vote, which is usually free in the sense that the People's Liberation Army liberated people. Tory mavericks, who had been summoned to the Whips' office to be told that of course they could vote howsoever they pleased, noticed two lists of rebellious Members, one headed 'Puritans', the other 'Cowards'. Why did they stop there? Why not throw in 'Greedheads', Slimeballs' or even 'Whipped Curs'?

There was one touching moment when Mr David Wilshire pleaded with the Speaker for help. Would she be kind enough to explain to MPs at each stage what, precisely, they were voting for? 'Normally we leave it to the great and the good, but on a free vote… ,' he said. The prospect of MPs actually having to know what they were voting about was indeed appalling, and Ms Boothroyd readily agreed to provide a crib.

Mr Tony Newton, the Leader of the House, spoke in the familiar mournful tones of a solicitor explaining that, while your millionaire uncle in South America has left you everything, 20 million escudos amounts to only £67. He explained that, under the new rules, MPs would not be allowed to accept any dosh at all for making speeches in the House, voting, or tabling parliamentary questions and amendments.

This all said with an air of appropriate gravity. But some of us had assumed as much already. What would be banned next? Demanding droit de seigneur from constituents' daughters? Murdering each other in exchange for trips abroad? Are we supposed to admire them and reward them for not being bent? Apparently so.

Sir Edward Heath declared that he was right. Why? we wondered. It turned out this was because he was right. In his view, MPs should not have to announce their private financial arrangements. 'So that argument has gone out of the window. What is the argument for disclosure? There is no argument,' he plonked.

Sir John Stanley made a short but moving speech. Mr Newton had said that Members who had financial interests should, when making a speech which touched on those interests, 'choose their words with care'. He for one had never chosen his words with care, and had no intention of starting now. It seemed a fitting epitaph for the whole debate.

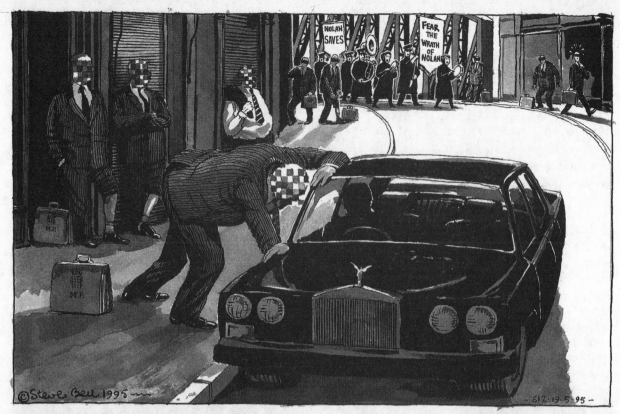

"THEY'RE ONLY GOING TO VOTE LABOUR, SO LET 'EM DIE"

46

See You in Court Sunbeam!

A Court of Law is to truth and justice what the House of Commons is to rational debate. Any which appears comes purely by chance, in the same way that the hundred monkeys with the hundred typewriters will occasionally produce a real word.

Recently I found myself in the High Court, helping my paper defend a libel action brought by Mr George Howarth, the Labour MP for Knowsley, near Liverpool. My article had wrongly implied that he was a bit of a rough diamond, without the diamond, and after two days of wrangling our side decided to back down. Mr Howarth left the court with a sum of money which I am not allowed to divulge, but which would enable him to buy a new car of such quality that if he were to leave it parked on a street in Merseyside, it would be stripped to its constituent parts in no time at all.

I learned two things from the experience. First, that a Court of Law is to truth and justice what the House of Commons is to rational debate. Any which appears comes purely by chance, in the same way that the hundred monkeys with the hundred typewriters will occasionally produce a real word.

Secondly, I learned that MPs' feelings are hurt just as easily as anyone else's. And why should they not be? If you were a teacher, or a butcher, or a personnel director, and every morning you woke up to find cruel mockery of your professional performance in the morning papers, you would be hurt too. You would be specially wounded if they read it out in the 'What the Papers Say' slot on breakfast TV: ' "Mr Figgis's display in the regular Tuesday sales meeting brought to mind Mr Pooter at the Lord Mayor's Ball – though without the same social poise," says the *Guardian*. And *The Times* is even more biting about Mr Figgis's report on sales in the South-west region…'

So in spite of my natural regret at losing the case, I did feel sorry for Mr Howarth. Sorry, but also inspired. During the trial, Mr Howarth remarked that, in his view, 'Hoggart is more nasty than funny.' The afternoon the case came to an end, I resolved to mend my ways.

I arrived in the Chamber just in time to hear Rachel Squire, the Labour Member for Dunfermline West, ask a question about registration and inspection procedures for nursing and residential homes in Scotland. I have rarely heard such a well-phrased question on that perenially fascinating subject.

The same went for the reply, furnished by James Douglas-Hamilton, a Junior Minister at the Scottish Office – junior now, but not for long, I fancy!

His answer covered many aspects of procedure for nursing and residential homes in Scotland with a thoroughness and a wealth of detail which won gasps of quiet – admittedly very quiet – admiration from all quarters of the House. Those of us who have been too ready to hold glib views on this important topic will perhaps have been forced to think again, and not before time!

Next we were enthralled by a statement from Virginia Bottomley, the Secretary of State for the National Heritage. As ever, 'Ginny' won the hearts of Members with her descriptions of the millennium exhibition at Greenwich, which we learned is to have the exciting name 'The Circle of Time'. It will be composed of twelve pavilions, all on the theme of time.

As Mrs Bottomley announced that the government's role in this event would be coordinated by Michael Heseltine, spontaneous cries of applause broke out. Here was yet another richly deserved title for our well-loved Deputy Prime Minister: First Time Lord!

Mrs Bottomley pointed out with her unfailing good humour that the last millennium had been presided over by Ethelred the Unready. Now, a thousand years later, we have another great monarch: Heseltine the Unbalanced.

Michael Jopling, the MP for Westmorland, pained those of us committed to the New Courtesy with an unkind reference to the city of Birmingham, some of whose representatives were upset because the fabled City of the River Chad has been passed over in favour of Greenwich. 'Northerners much prefer London to Birmingham, which they think of as somewhere you go through on the way to London,' he said, with just the faintest edge of churlishness, one felt.

Thank heavens for Mrs Bottomley, who quickly restored the mood of good fellowship which we have come to expect from the Commons. 'Perhaps you are unduly harsh on the joys of Birmingham,' she said. 'It certainly is a magnificent city!'

To me, as a Born Again Sketchwriter, the saddest moment came while she was making a series of moving remarks about the National Lottery. Her eyes raised to a vision of the future, she said, 'The Lottery provides the means by which the dreams and aspirations of the people of this country can find their realisation!'

As we pondered the profundity of this thought, the harsh voice of George Foulkes, Labour MP for Carrick, cut through our reverie. 'What a load of garbage!' he shouted. Has this oaf not heard of the new guidelines?

The Schoolboy of The Western World

I'M A FULL TIME BASTARD!

As so often when one listens to Michael Portillo, the mind reels gently, like a drunk pitching from one wall to another.

Michael Portillo does not like people discussing his Spanish background. He detests it when they jokily use the Spanish pronunciation of his name, Por-*ti*-yo, regarding it as a cheap slur on his British allegiance. Introduced to a young woman at a party, he was told, 'You'll have a lot to talk about, because she is half-Spanish too.' Portillo turned his back without a word. Recently an interviewer suggested that his Spanish background might give him an intriguing perspective on European problems. 'And what is that supposed to mean?' he snapped. 'I am as British as you are.'

Yet it would be astonishing if his revered Spanish father had not had some effect on him, quite apart from giving him his distinctive Mediterranean appearance. He does not slouch like so many British politicians; instead he is smartly dressed and walks with a swaggering confidence, so that an ordinary jacket and trousers on him might be a suit of lights.

He is also a Jesuit by inclination if not by training. Jesuits had the job in the Roman Catholic Church of finding rational arguments to support irrational faith. This is invaluable in politics, and the skills came in handy when he defended the government's decision to sell off service families' housing. This move, disadvantageous to the public and to the families, highly lucrative for the successful bidder, had angered many Conservative back-benchers, who saw it as a means of chiselling tax cuts at the expense of the services.

With a skill which would have pleased the Inquisition, Mr Portillo suggested that it was the very fact that Conservatives were objecting to the sale which proved that it was right:

'I'm not surprised that it was Conservatives who raised the questions. It's the Conservative Party that cares about defence, and knows the issues that are of interest to service families.'

As so often when one listens to Michael Portillo, the mind reels gently, like a drunk pitching from one wall to another. If Tory doubts about the sale prove that it was the Tories who really care about our boys, doesn't that show the sale is mistaken? Or, if it is such a splendid idea, why does the Caring Party object so loudly?

There came no answer, but that did not matter. Conservative MPs resemble monastic novices. Being young, they are plagued by the terrors of Doubt. Yet being ambitious too, they wish to have their faith untroubled and secure. Cardinal Xavier is able to offer them that security. No wonder they all meekly voted for the sale of service homes at the end of the debate, lulled back into the warm embrace of the Mother Party.

I had been told that one could not understand Michael Portillo without going to Spain, so I made a pilgrimage to the family home of Madrigal de las Altas Torres. The village is cramped and poor, the land around it almost barren, occupied only by a few straggling herds of sheep. The Portillo family moved here in the sixteenth century. As befits the home of a great statesman, Madrigal used to be a place of immense consequence in the world. It was the site of King Juan II of Castile's summer palace, and was the birthplace of Queen Isabella, who despatched Columbus to the New World.

Michael, who is known locally by the diminutive 'Miguelito' – roughly the equivalent of Mickey – used to come here for his holidays almost every year. Now most of the family has moved away, though cousin Adolfo still lives in Madrigal. He has the family nose and thick fleshy lips – not so much beestung, but looking as if the owner teased hornets as a hobby – and the same pile of slicked-back hair, though this is presumably not genetic.

Portillo's grandfather, Don Justino, put all his seven sons through university at Salamanca, which is sixty miles away and before the War was Spain's equivalent of Oxbridge. The town has two of the finest cathedrals in the world and it is impossible to sit in the 'new' cathedral – the last great Gothic building in Europe – gazing awestruck at the towers, the cupolas and the light surging through the stained glass on to the gold inside, without thinking to oneself, 'Michael Portillo would have demanded private-sector funding for this.'

Portillo's father Luis was a socialist, and opposed Franco in the Spanish Civil War. He worked as a civil servant in the Justice Department, and it is said he helped find excuses for not executing prisoners on the other side. His son's followers have, perhaps, slightly tweaked his importance: he is said to have been a friend of the great poet Lorca, though none of Lorca's biographers have noted the connection, and he appears only as one small footnote in Hugh Thomas's history of the War. Afterwards, Franco arranged for the death of uncounted thousands from the Republican side. By then, Luis had fled to Britain, where he married a Scottish socialist called Cora. Their son, at one time an enthusiastic Labour supporter himself, must have learned the vital importance of not being on the losing side in politics.

In Spain they are somewhat

mystified by Portillo's extraordinary chauvinism, to use the word in its true sense. The paper *El Pais* accused him of wearing 'xenophobic plumage' after a speech in which he declared that only British academic qualifications had any meaning, since those abroad were obtained by cheating. His support for Margaret Thatcher mystifies them, too; the lesson she learned from the past was that consensus is always fatal. The lesson they have imbibed is that only consensus is essential to prevent terrible bloodshed.

A few days after I had returned from Spain, Michael Portillo made his annual speech to the Conservative Party conference. This was three months after it had been revealed that, while pledging public support to John Major, he had arranged for two dozen phone lines to be installed to facilitate his attempt to become Party leader in the second round.

His speech was greeted with foot-stamping ecstacy by the conference – or at least by the short-haired young men in dark suits who are Mr Portillo's most enthusiastic followers. It met less acclaim from his fellow MPs, who will one day choose their next leader.

It was an anti-Brussels rant, of course. He could turn the welcome at a Tupperware party into an anti-Brussels rant. It was also rather childish – the voice of a schoolboy bragging about his toys: 'Three letters send a chill down the spine of the enemy – SAS. Those letters spell out one clear message: Don't mess with Britain!' he said, snarling. Only three nations, including our own, would have Tomahawk missiles, 'so accurate that they can be launched from a

submarine a thousand miles away and guided down a single chimney!'

He declared that Labour had not truly changed its mind on CND. 'Anyone, they say, is entitled to change his mind. Not about the defence of Britain, you're not. You either feel it in your heart, in your bones, in your gut, or you don't!'

How appropriate that the very day he made this speech we learned from his biographer that Miguelito was such a pacifist in his youth, as to refuse to join the school cadet corps. So clearly he doesn't feel it in his gut. In his hairdo, perhaps.

He ended by quoting the SAS motto, 'Who dares, wins' – though it was Mr John Redwood who actually dared to stand against the Prime Minister. Maybe the cap badge should be rewritten: 'Who dares, installs phone lines.' Either way, I had the vivid image of Mr Portillo being launched from a submarine, then dropped, with astonishing accuracy, down a chimney a thousand miles away.

THE HAUNTING

One is reminded of Canova's Three Graces, perhaps, except they should be the Three Disgraces, or more appropriately the Three Miseries. They are locked together, all right, frozen in time, but instead of caressing each other in a faintly Sapphic, yet pubescent manner, they are ruthlessly stabbing each other in the back.

Sir Edward Heath loathes Lady Thatcher. He also holds Mr Major in a profound contempt. Lady Thatcher in turn holds him in even deeper disregard. Mr Major somehow manages to conceal his own loathing, in public at least, though those who know him well say that Lady Thatcher sometimes brings him near to despair.

As one Tory MP said, 'They have a mutual loathing. And all three of them are right.'

Lady Thatcher never misses a chance to be rude about Mr Major in her memoirs. (These constitute her celebrated backwards autobiography. The years as Prime Minister came first, then her rise from mere childhood to supreme power, and finally we should be served with *Volume III: Foetus of Destiny*.)

The constant drip of her hatred. The joy and the cheering among her supporters on the last election night when John Major's best friend Chris Patten lost his seat in Bath ('another Conservative gain!') She is the opposite of one of those people who, tediously, fall in love and miss no opportunity to bore everybody else about the object of their adoration. Their obsessiveness blinds them to the fact that other people may want to talk about something else, anything else – the weather, the football scores, the presumption of compatibility – anything at all.

Talking to a man from the BBC's innumerable political staff, she asked about the twice-weekly broadcast of Prime Minister's Question Time. 'I gather that the ratings have fallen dramatically since 1980,' she said with a smile of slight but bitter satisfaction. Another BBC interviewer asked her about John Major's legacy. She praised him on camera, by saying in effect that all his achievements had been the result of her own

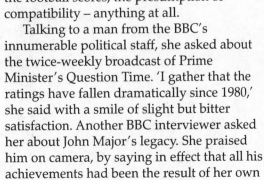

Sir Edward Heath loathes Lady Thatcher. He also holds Mr Major in a profound contempt. Lady Thatcher in turn holds him in even deeper disregard. Mr Major somehow manages to conceal his own loathing, in public at least, though those who know him well say that Lady Thatcher sometimes brings him near to despair.

hard work, courage and wisdom. The interviewer tried to probe further. 'I think I have said quite enough nice things about John Major,' she declared, and got herself ready to go.

Surrounded by those who agree with her, such as her husband, she cannot conceive that Mr Major might have a point, that one reason his job is impossible to do is the legacy she left him. When Bill Cash, a Tory MP, was told that he could not accept money from Sir James Goldsmith, who proposed to put up parliamentary candidates against Conservatives, she promptly filled the gap, writing a cheque herself, declaring in effect that she was now more important than the success of the Party she had once led.

Edward Heath cuts a lonely figure, shuttling from his home in Salisbury to London, to Europe, and to Moonies' conventions in Washington, accompanied only by his detectives. He has two moods: playful exhilaration, or an aggressive sort of gloominess. She is brought down by external events: her son's tribulations, all self-inflicted, her illnesses. Lady Thatcher is told by those she knows that she is always right and remains irreplaceable. Mr Major has to tell himself, and all those around him, constantly.

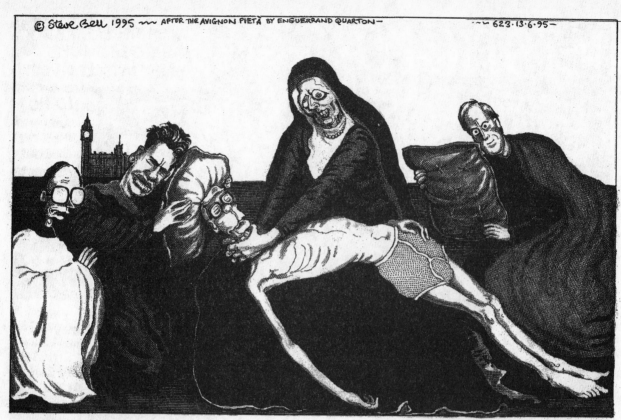

© Steve Bell 1995 — AFTER THE AVIGNON PIETÀ BY ENGUERRAND QUARTON — ~~ 623·13·6·95 —

NHS EXISTS OFFICIAL

© Steve Bell 1996 ~ 711·12·1·96 —

News from Nutwood

There is a long and honourable tradition of Members of Parliament being bonkers. Mostly they are Tories. There are a few Labour loonies, but only a handful are loony enough to make the grade.

There is a long and honourable tradition of Members of Parliament being bonkers. Mostly they are Tories. There are a few Labour loonies, but only a handful are loony enough to make the grade. Most are lawyers, teachers, trade union officials, having occupied dreary but sane jobs in real life.

One popular loony is Tam Dalyell, a man of many obsessions. Quite often he is right in his obsessions, but it seems to be a matter of chance, as if you were to believe passionately, with every fibre of your being, that a tossed coin will come up tails. You can often tell a loony by his diet. Tony Benn, for example, lives on mugs of tea and sandwiches. He assumes that the working classes, the backbone of our nation, subsist on similar fare, whereas in fact they rightly prefer smoked salmon roulades followed by steak. The late Sir Keith Joseph used to be invited to expensive restaurants by journalists. As they ordered for themselves the expensive specialities of the house, he would ask if he might have some cake – 'British Rail cake,' he would add, meaning the slabs of dense fruit cake which used to be sold on trains.

Tam is a boiled egg man, and rarely goes far without his supply. MPs and candidates are always warned while canvassing that they should never accept the numerous cups of tea they will be offered; not only does this waste precious time, but it means that soon afterwards you will be forced to ask to use another voter's toilet, which could create an over-familiar impression. However on one occasion, while canvassing in Scotland, Tam bemused his helpers by accepting the offer of tea, then pulled two eggs from his pocket and said, 'And would you mind boiling these?' He does understand that other people may need something more substantial. He once famously entertained the late Eric Heffer, who had been speaking in his constituency. There was no mention of food either before or after the meeting. Tam then welcomed him back to stay at his ancestral home, The Binns, and took the now famished Heffer on a guided tour. As they walked through the cellars, they passed a dead cow, hanging from a hook. 'Are you hungry?' asked Tam, 'because if you are, cut yourself a slice off that.'

Mr Tony Banks, the Labour Member for Newham, is a comedian, and a funny one. But in his case this is a deliberate act. So it is too with Mr Jerry Hayes, the Tory MP, whose ambition it is to appear on every single television programme, from the *Open University* to *Supermarket Sweep*. So great is Mr Hayes's passion for publicity that he has even performed stand-up comedy at Butlins holiday camp in Pwllheli, telling jokes about his colleagues. ('So David Mellor goes to see the doctor about his halitosis. "Dear me, that is a bad case," says the doctor. "What you have to do is take some horse manure, rub it all round your face, inside your mouth, over your lips, really work it into the tongue." "Will that cure it?" asks Mellor. "No," says the doctor, "but it will take the edge off." ')

The true eccentric is an MP who does not realise how strange he is, who assumes that his behaviour is perfectly normal in the eyes of ordinary people. Take Mr Jacques (pronounced 'Jakes') Arnold, the Conservative Member for Gravesham, or the Unquiet Gravesham as we now call it.

Mr Arnold has the voice of a skeleton gargling. It is dry and dusty, like rats scuttling behind a wainscot. As he stands up from the back benches, his face white, his hair black, his body stooped, I am reminded of T. S. Eliot's poem: 'We are the hollow men / We are the stuffed men / Leaning together / Headpiece filled with straw. Alas.'

My theory is that Mr Arnold is one of the Undead. Every morning at daybreak, the duty Whip has the job of burying him in a coffin in unconsecrated ground near Cheapside. When night falls, and his vote is required, they dig him up again and bring him in a chauffeur-driven hearse (well, you could hardly have a self-drive hearse) back to the Commons. As he rises in his place, bits of soil fall from his matted locks. Once he supported John Redwood for the party leadership, but the Whips threatened him with garlic and silver crucifixes, so now he always performs their bidding, speaking like a Haitian zombie, all will extinguished by their power.

These days his questions are so oily, so thick and greasy and lustrous, that they could serve as Swarfega industrial cleanser. 'Will you agree with me that the firm and resolute management of the British economy by this government has created the best-performing economy in Europe?' he asks, challengingly, as if liable to be contradicted by the Prime Minister.

That poser would have been thought quite adequate by some of Parliament's most accomplished sycophants. But Mr Arnold cannot be halted. Like a sleepwalker, he knows no fear and senses no danger: '...does he agree that it would be a tragedy if this were to be thrown away by a Labour government...' he droned on. At least Boris Karloff's voice went up and down a bit: 'An icicle, inserted in the brain, will melt, and leave no trace.' Mr Arnold's voice is entirely flat, as he lives his half-life somewhere between consciousness and sleep.

Another Member with an extraordinary voice is Dame Elaine Kellett-Bowman, who sits in the Conservative interest for Lancaster. This is so high-pitched that on occasion only bats, and some Liberal Democrats, can hear it. If Dame Elaine were dishonest, bookmakers would pay her to stand at race courses. By shouting at the favourite as it thundered home, she could make it drop dead, like Devon Loch in the Grand National, while remaining inaudible to the authorities. Air-traffic control computers at Heathrow have been known to go down when Mrs Kellett-Bowman is particularly angry. The voice is said to have miraculous powers: it can make the blind deaf.

For these reasons we do not always know when Dame Elaine is attempting to take part in a debate. The voice exists somewhere on the edge of our consciousness, as in a dream, when we imagine ourselves trapped inside a burning building and wake to realise that the clanging bell is only our alarm clock. And like an alarm clock, she is persistent – though without the convenient 'snooze' button which would enable us to switch her off for ten more minutes.

It was Dame Elaine's remarkable tenacity, coupled with her complete absence of a sense of humour, which caused her to save Harriet Harman in her first debate since it was learned that the then Labour health spokeswoman planned to send her son to a selective school.

Ms Harman had ignored all the Dame's attempts to intervene in her speech. The voice dipped and swooped, then soared higher, like a Mosquito jet. Somewhere a flying saucer from the Planet Thaarggh, whose occupants had been planning to kidnap Jacques Arnold and extract his bodily fluids, found their navigation system had crashed, and flew home instead.

The Dame kept demanding that Harriet give way. At one point she screamed 'Sexist!' across the Chamber, and all the milk in the catering department instantly went off.

She tried again. And then again. Finally she rose on a point of order. 'Is it in order,' she demanded, 'for the honourable lady to practise SEX DISCRIMINATION?' At this point the atomic clock at Greenwich stopped for a nano-second.

Ms Harman paused briefly. 'It isn't sex discrimination which makes me not respond to the honourable lady's intervention. It is kindness.'

Not a dazzling joke by any means, but passable in parliamentary terms. The beauty of it was that it saved Ms Harman's day (she went on to be voted back into the Shadow Cabinet – just) but it left the Dame entirely unaffected. One reason may be that she herself finds it impossible to hear normal speech.

If you asked most Tory MPs who the looniest of their number was, many would give you the name of George Walden, the MP for Buckingham. Mr Walden, who used to be a very senior official at the Foreign Office, is probably the nearest thing the Tory Party has to an intellectual, unless you include Mr David Willetts, the deeply serious Junior Minister who has the intense, glazed look of all clever people whose brains have been given over to the service of political propaganda.

Mr Walden is not interested in political propaganda, which makes him almost unique among MPs. He believes that politicians lie to the voters, persuading them, for electoral purposes, that their problems are modest and easily solved. He is also a great reader, preferring social realism and detesting the Merchant-Ivory view of Britain. This he believes contributes to our great national delusion, that soon the glory days of the Edwardian era will return, and once again we will sit in our rightful place on the top table of nations. Clearly Mr Walden has little connection with the modern Conservative Party.

Once he defended Jack Straw, who had made some more or less critical observations about the Royal Family. Mr Walden wondered whether it is 'grown-up politics, or for that matter, intelligent politics, for Ministers to hunt him like a pack of demented corgis? Do you think that we, as a Party, can hope to reconcile the encouragement of indiscriminate deference towards well-born nonentities...'

It took a while for the dimmer Labour Members to twig that this was an attack on the Royals. You could almost hear the noise, like a old, wheezing air conditioner, as their brains changed direction: '...with our policy of promoting social parity in this country?'

It was Mr Walden who was first on his feet to abuse the Prime Minister after his patched-up deal with Europe on beef. Was he aware, he asked, that his policy of vetoing everything had caused Britain to lose prestige, money and umpteen thousand cows? He had allowed himself to be pushed into a mistaken policy by the 'petty chauvinism' of the Press. 'If we feel big after that, we must have been feeling rather small before,' he said, dripping with contempt.

It is not surprising that Mr Walden has decided to quit the House of Commons at the next election. In an elegaic farewell to his constituents, he said ruefully that one of his colleagues had described him as being 'as useful as a flat cap in a submarine'. The phrase was familiar, yet puzzling. If you needed protection from rain in a submarine, presumably it was already too late. But if you did need headgear for some reason, a flat cap would seem to be ideal.

Then I remembered its origin. I had quoted the remark, which had been made to me by a right-wing Tory. 'George Walden,' he said, 'is as useful as a cat flap in a submarine.' This made more sense, yet in a way I preferred Mr Walden's own version, which has a certain surrealist charm.

The quintessential opposite to Mr Walden is Mr David Evans, the Conservative MP for Welwyn, and a member of the Executive of the 1922 Committee, which means, in the unreal world of modern politics, that we are obliged to take him seriously.

Mr Evans is a businessman, and in some mysterious fashion he seems to believe that this puts him in touch with the common man. (In the past it was farm labourers, or factory workers, who were thought to be representative of ordinary folk, in that they themselves were ordinary folk. Now we are supposed to follow those who exploit ordinary folk. The likes of Mr Rupert Murdoch or his satraps are truly representative of the commonality, since they make millions out of them.)

Mr Evans has been trying (and failing) to make a well-loved national character out of his wife, Janice. His contributions to the proceedings tended to recount Janice's robust, commonsense declamations. For example, 'Janice 'ad a shock this morning, when she read in the *GUARDIAN* that David Evans 'ad been sponsoring BAMBI...' This was a reference to another David Evans who had given financial support to Mr Blair, and was clearly fake; one could never picture Janice, in a pink nylon baby doll nightie, sitting up in bed and reading the *Guardian*, or anything else except the *Sun*.

'Unlike the Pa'ay opposite,' he will boom, 'we are all to'ally united behind AAR LEA'ER! Larst Fursday, BAMBI showed the nation on live television, what we 'ave known on this si'e for years, that they are all to'ally incom'etent, in ovver words, Men of Straw!' This too was a fib, since Mr Evans had supported John Redwood a few months earlier.

Sometimes Mr Evans likes to turn proceedings into a kind of party game. 'Worrit a Conserrr-vative gummint that le' inflition rip at 26.9 per cent?' A few of the sillier Tories shout 'No-o-o!' 'Was it the Conserrr-vatives allahed the higher ray of tax to gerrup to 98 per cent in the pahnd?' He ploughed wearisomely through more rhetorical questions, until the Speaker interrupted to say that it was no wonder that she received so many complaints about Question Time in her morning mailbag.

By now the joke has worn thin. When Mr Evans rises, with another carefully prepared emotional rant, even the Tories react with grudging tolerance and wish that he would stop.

My own favourite loony of all is Michael Fabricant, the Tory MP for Mid-Staffordshire. Dr Fabricant (he has a PhD in something or other) is best known for his hair. This is a strawberry blond colour and it shines lustrously. It may even shine in the dark. It resembles whatever substance it is they use to make tails for My Little Pony.

Tory MPs are deeply divided about whether this is a wig or not. It is a subject of continuous speculation, and many MPs take sides, rather like Swift's big-enders and little-enders. Some argue that it must be a wig, and to suggest that such a bizarre confection could be the result of natural growth indicates extreme naïveté. Their rivals point out that the hair appears to grow and then be cut back; the Wig Party poo-poohs this, pointing out that these days people buy hairpieces of different lengths, in order to persuade onlookers that their tresses are real. The anti-Wiggites say that nobody would conceivably buy a toupee which looked like that; it is its complete lack of resemblance to anything like normal human hair which proves that it must be real.

Dr Strangelocks refuses to say for certain, contenting himself with runic remarks such as 'Things are not always what they seem,' which could confirm either theory, and in any case might be a double bluff. Since I have started writing about him, I have begun to receive many letters concerning him and his ways – almost all of them anonymous. One, from someone claiming to be a constituent, says that in his early days as an MP he was so hurt by the allegations of wig wearing that he offered to jump out of a plane, with a parachute but without a helmet, in order to prove that the hair was real. For some reason, he was dissuaded.

There is something quite engagingly mad about Mr Fabricant. He is a greaser – without doubt one of the worst in the House – yet his enthusiasm is so enormous one might almost believe that he believes the glutinous rubbish which he spouts. Indeed he is so carried away on occasion that he has to be rebuked.

On a day when he has a question tabled, Mr Fabricant is a-quiver with excitement. One imagines him casually dropping the fact, on the phone to friends, or at the bus stop with total strangers. 'Yes, as a matter of fact, I do have a question tabled today for the President of the Board of Trade, since you ask. I plan to put him on the spot with a no-holds-barred query about his plans to visit the United States for talks about free trade. He won't wriggle out of that one, I'll be bound!'

Then lunch, almost impossible to eat. Taking one's seat (almost exactly below mine, a few feet above in the Press Gallery). The agony, as question two follows number one, followed in turn by three, then inexorably but oh so slowly, number four. At times like this Mr Fabricant's entire body is devoted to what psychologists call 'displacement activities'. He knits his fingers together, as if making a cat's cradle. He fans himself with his order paper, puts it first to one side and then the other, after which he pulls out a set of keys to jingle, absent-mindedly. He makes a chin strap out of his hands and inserts his chin. Sometimes he twitches in a slow, almost formal manner, rather like those exercises they suggest you do during long flights. Then finally, just in time, the moment he had longed for. 'Mr Fabricant!' called the Speaker. 'Number fourteen!' shouted Mr Fabricant in reply.

Mr Ian Lang, the President of the Board of Trade, said that he would be going to the United States before too long. Then Mr Fabricant blew it. He was like the triangle player who has one note to perform in the entire symphony and then misses his entry. He said that he was 'delighted' Mr Lang would be going to America. He was delighted that he would be visiting Canada, as well, 'a united Canada, I might say'. He discussed how the US is our second largest trading partner, and the fact that Britain is the largest foreign investor there.

It all came burbling out. The pent-up excitement, the planning, the nervous energy. Our shared culture! Our common language! Our common legal system (the one which got O. J. Simpson off, he didn't add). Aeons of geological time seemed to pass. Then, majestically,

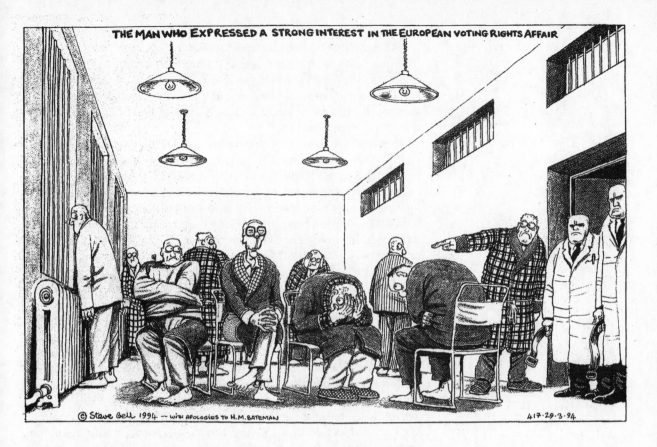

THE MAN WHO EXPRESSED A STRONG INTEREST IN THE EUROPEAN VOTING RIGHTS AFFAIR

© Steve Bell 1994 ~ WITH APOLOGIES TO H.M.BATEMAN

417·29·3·94

the Speaker rose. 'I must adjourn the debate on this interesting topic. Perhaps you will now put your question, or else resume your seat.'

Mr Fabricant tried to make light of it. 'I stand chastised,' he said in what he hoped was a jovial manner. But we knew that all had been lost. Like an Olympic athlete, disqualified at the start after four years of training, his life lay temporarily in ruins.

Some of the letters I receive concerning Mr Fabricant are signed by him and written in green ink. These I assume are forgeries. Others are allegedly from spies, at Westminster and in his constituency. Sometimes they enclose newspaper clippings, showing Mr Fabricant in silly clothes performing some stunt for charity. One told me that he had been seen driving a Ford 'Probe', a car possessed only by travelling salesmen who think it will attract women. Some of these letters end by pointing out that Mr Fabricant is really a decent, intelligent, amusing kind of fellow, 'but you don't want to know that, do you?'

Of course I don't. It would spoil everything. Such letters merely persuade me that they have been written by Mr Fabricant himself; by giving me shiny new nuggets to print, he hopes to slide in a few meagre words of praise. It doesn't work.

These days Mr Fabricant has become a well-loved parliamentary character, like a favourite barmaid or wise-cracking policeman. His fellow MPs were delighted when they watched the BBC series *The Final Cut*, a political thriller. It was full of solecisms – MPs asking questions while sitting down, Cabinet Ministers plonked on the back

63

benches, and many others. All was explained by the final credits: 'Political Adviser: Michael Fabricant MP.'

I fear now that Mr Fabricant and I have been locked together, doomed to wrestle each other to death, like Holmes and Moriarty. He, I know, is obsessed. Once he burst into the Members' Tea Room, stormed up to a table full of Labour MPs, and demanded to know why I was picking on him.

'Because you keep writing to him, you pillock,' said Dale Campbell-Savours, demonstrating an admirable understanding of the sketchwriter's trade. Yet nothing stops him. Listed to ask a question about the effect of government policies on the people of Lichfield – his next constituency – he will list the innumerable benefits these have brought, pausing only to add that businesses have been inconvenienced by the postal strike – called by a union which provides financial support for some Labour MPs! I once made some inquiries in Lichfield about the real problems businesses faced there: these turned out to include crime, up by 140 per cent since the Conservatives had returned to office, foreign investment being withdrawn, increased business rents, and so forth, none of them things ever mentioned by Mr Fabricant.

The sense that he and I are doomed to be linked forever in some parliamentary hell was strengthened when Dr Fabricant introduced a bill designed to make it easier for people the fly the Union Jack. This turned out to be a disguised attack on Labour plans for devolution. For once his speech was answered rather than ignored. Mr Tony Banks told him, 'No one has greased more assiduously than you, as you carry any political lunchbox... You will kiss the bottom of any passing authority... You are not an incipient Minister, but a wretched youth congratulating himself on getting the last cabin boy's job on the *Titanic*. All your bill does is provide more cheap copy for Simon Hoggart.'

I have never met him, but we support each other's careers. When I stop writing about him for a spell, I get readers' letters asking for more Fabricant news. And he was promoted. He is now PPS to a Junior Treasury Minister, the first handhold on the greasy pole to power.

TO PIECES IN OUR TIME

In Ulster the term 'peace' is merely shorthand for 'peace on our terms'. Nothing ever truly changes.

The Troubles in Northern Ireland have been continuing now for nearly thirty years. Since they began, the pound has lost nearly ninety per cent of its value, the United States has had six Presidents, and Ulster itself has had nine Secretaries of State – governors without the plumage, or indeed the power.

There are two great myths about the place. The first, trotted out every time there is another outrage, is that the IRA are 'cowardly'. No, they're not. They might be wicked, misguided, futile, sadistic – all these things. But they are courageous. One-twentieth of the death rate in their line of work would be unacceptable in any other, and a far higher proportion of their numbers end up in jail than, say, burglars.

What we tend to forget is that being in the IRA is a family thing, as it often is with greengrocers and gypsies, except that in their case it is the fanaticism which is passed on down the line. When I worked in Northern Ireland I went out for some months with a beautiful young schoolteacher from an old IRA family. Her uncle was in jail

for being a member of the IRA. Her aunt was in jail for recruiting people to the IRA, and was later assassinated in her hospital bed. Her cousin had blown himself up while bombing a set of council offices; he was killed, but pathetically, the 'Paisley for Prime Minister' pen he had left at the scene to make it appear the work of Protestants had been saved. Her brother was periodically beaten up by British soldiers because of his surname.

Yet she did not appear to mind too much. In her family, death was always imminent. Death was part of the job, just like VAT returns. Complaining was as pointless as a footballer whinging that people kept kicking his shins. Even the families in our own armed forces are inclined to be less philosophical than Irish Republicans. We ought to understand this, even while we condemn what they have done, and despise their utter failure to recognise reality.

The other myth beloved in Parliament is that the people of Northern Ireland want peace. No, they don't; they want victory. If they wanted peace, they could vote for peace. They could vote,

for example, for the Alliance Party, which usually gets between ten and twelve per cent of the poll, and got just over six per cent in the last elections. People pooh-pooh the Alliance Party as a collection of middle-class do-gooders, yet no gutsy 'relevant' working-class peace party ever arises to take its place.

In Ulster the term 'peace' is merely shorthand for 'peace on our terms'. Nothing ever truly changes. The Protestants accept nothing which might satisfy the Nationalist cravings; the Republicans will accept nothing which will not move towards a United Ireland. The present Troubles began in 1968 when Orangemen wanted to march through Catholic parts of Derry; twenty-eight years later precisely the same arguments were being rehearsed.

Tell the people there and their elected representatives that this is absurd and disgusting and that the world has moved on, and they become puzzled and resentful, as if you were to argue that the Football League had had ample opportunity to decide which was the best club and should stop playing matches forthwith.

© Steve Bell 1996 ~ AFTER THE PHOTO © IAN BRADSHAW · ~ 726·13·2·96 ~

© Steve Bell 1996 ~ · ~ 730·20·2·96 ~

"United Republican Struggle"

74

It is an article of faith among many Scottish people that their concerns are ignored at Westminster. The English, they complain, have neither interest in nor understanding of Scotland.

It is an article of faith among many Scottish people that their concerns are ignored at Westminster. The English, they complain (and one has the impression that they imagine the English as effete chinless persons in rowing blazers, drinking Pimm's at a marquee in Henley) have neither interest in nor understanding of Scotland.

This is true. We don't. For the most part, we couldn't care less. But it makes no difference. There are times when the House of Commons seems to discuss very little except Scotland. Apart from the one-hour Scottish Question Time every month, longer than the sessions devoted to other parts of the kingdom, there are rambling debates on new laws which apply only to Scotland, endless discussion of devolution and independence, combined with a constant, general sucking-up to Scotland by all sides.

The Scots have become adept filibusterers. Mr Alex Salmond, the leader of the Scottish National Party, contrived to keep a debate about the Standing Committee on the Education (Scotland) Bill going for hours. In this country, unlike the United States Congress,

BEIGEHEART – THE CHOICE FOR SCOTLAND

legislators are obliged to stick more or less to the subject nominally under debate. This makes the art of the filibuster far more difficult than it is on Capitol Hill. It becomes like that radio game, *Just A Minute*, retitled *Just a Couple of Hours* and with repetition not only allowed, but positively encouraged. One can only admire Mr Salmond's pluck and determination. Robert the Bruce could have learned much from him, and the spider would have given up and gone home hours before.

Meanwhile, Scots are over-represented among MPs, which means that they have more influence over English affairs than the English do over Scotland. (One of the last Tory MPs north of the border was a man called David Myles, who sat for Banff. He once tried to get a drink from the chap who was known as the Rudest Barman in Westminster. As he placed his order, this rough fellow inquired, 'Are you a Member?' He replied, 'I'm Myles, from Banff.' 'Aren't we all?' said the Rudest Barman. 'I arst if you was a Member.'

Scots are wildly over-represented in the upper reaches of the three main Parties. Though the Tories now have only eleven Scottish MPs, no fewer than three of them – Lang, Rifkind and Forsyth – are in the Cabinet. Two of Labour's big three, Brown and Cook, sit for Scottish seats and Blair is of Scottish descent. There are three other Scots in the Shadow Cabinet, including the Chief Whip. Far from being a dispossessed forgotten colony, a sort of Tristan da Cunha within the United Kingdom, the Scots seem close to running the place.

CENTRAL EUROPEAN BIZTIME PRODUCTIONS PRESENTS

LOW McNOON

DO NOT FORRRSAKE ME OH MA DARRRLINN....

Featuring the HIT SHOWSTOPPERS: 'It serves you right for living so far North' + 'PORRIDGE IN THE DARK'

Meanwhile, the two largest Parties are now like weak parents with a spoiled adolescent child. They give way to almost every demand, whether for a new car or their own assembly, desperate for their offspring not to walk out of the door and start a new life.

They are helped by the incontrovertible fact – so agonising to many Scots – that the English are not interested in Scottish affairs. For many English people their one encounter with Scottish culture ended when Andy Stewart stopped hosting the White Heather Club. Some in the Labour Party seem to imagine that the English would be desperately jealous of a Scottish assembly and would demand regional parliaments of their own. The fact is that most English people show not the faintest concern. If there ever is a Scottish Parliament, they will ignore it. To the average citizen of, say, Wigan, Scotland is famous for three things: 1) Billy Connolly came from there, 2) Paul Gascoigne played there, and 3) it is the land that invented the deep-fried Mars Bar.

Back at Westminster, however, Scottish affairs worm their way into almost every debate. References to any facet of Scottish life or culture call forth a stream of cringing praise. A mention of Rabbie Burns is usually sufficient to bring debate to a crashing halt, as it did when Mr Phil Gallie, the Tory MP for Ayr, stood up during Education Questions to complain that the new crop of post office stamps featuring quotes from the poet contained misspellings. He was distinctly agitated.

Of course they contained misspellings. Burns was like the

Guardian in the bad old days. Spelling was haphazard and depended largely on the goodwill and perceptual skills of the reader. Even when the words were correctly spelled, they didn't mean anything: 'for the sake of old long since', for example.

I expect that you, like me, imagined that 'Scots wha hae!' was a meaningless exhortation, like 'Allez, France!' In fact, it is short for 'Scots wha hae wi' Wallace bled', and it is like shouting out 'Scots who have!' at a football match.

Mr Gallie's distress concerned the 19p stamp, which quoted the poem 'To a Mouse'. The Post Office records the opening line as 'Wee, sleeket, cowran, tim'rous beastie', whereas some authorities prefer 'wee, sleeket, coweran, tim'rous beastie' – as if it made the slightest difference.

And while we're on the subject, what on earth is an 'honest, sonsie face'? Or a 'cog o'guid swats'? Or 'I gie them a skelp'? 'Monie jobs that day begin, may end in houghmagandie' cannot possibly mean anything at all.

'Whistle o'er the lave o't' is the first line of a poem mysteriously titled 'Whistle o'er the lave o't'. One of the more gripping passages of 'Tam O'Shanter' reads, 'Till ilka carlin swat and reekit, / And coost her duddies to the wark.'

There is an important difference between Mr Gallie and Rabbie Burns. Mr Gallie is a rough, untutored fellow who is posing as a Conservative MP and therefore a toff. Rabbie Burns was a toff who posed as a rough, untutored peasant. Either way, it is impossible to say anything rude about him at all, especially if you are an English MP – and nobody did.

But if the Scots dislike the English, they tend to detest each other. Scottish politics is quite separate and distinct from English politics, even if at times the two might appear, to the casual observer, to be overlapping. To describe Scottish politics as a snake pit would be unfair to snakes, who seem to get on fairly well, and just sort of slither over each other. Either way, 'slithering' may well be Scots dialect for slitting someone with a Stanley knife: 'Awa' an' raffle yer doughnut, sonny, or else ah'll sleether ye!' (Or as one Glaswegian Tory agent – a rare breed – once put it, 'If at first ye don't succeed / In wi' the boot and in wi' the heid!')

They all hate each other. Gordon Brown hates Robin Cook and Robin Cook hates Gordon Brown. Mr Cook also shares a mutual dislike with his old debating adversary from Edinburgh student days, Malcolm Rifkind. Everyone hates George Galloway. Even lovable folk heroes such as the Georges Foulkes and Robertson have their enemies, someone who will invariably tak' the high road if they see some other Scot takkin' the low road, even if it's only as far as the tea room.

At Scottish Question Time there is a permanent, low, gutteral grumbling. Each contribution is met by a sound not unlike a cesspit emptying, or else by vowel sounds rarely heard south of the Border. There is a constant crossness in the atmosphere. This may have something to do with the diet and particularly the deep-fried Mars Bars. (These are dipped in batter before being plunged into the fat. At the classier type of Scottish restaurant you can have it served

either as an entree or as the main course.)

They snarl at each other all the time. Mr John Home Robertson who, though he is a distant relation of the late Lord Home, is a Labour MP, called the Secretary of State 'a little Englander from Stirling'. Mr Forsyth called attention to Mr Home Robertson's wealth, which derives from cattle farming: 'No doubt he has plenty of fat to help him through the crisis.'

In the midst of this ill humour sometimes steps the stooped and courteous figure of Lord James Douglas-Hamilton, a Minister who may be the only Scottish politician to be liked by all other Scottish politicians. This is probably because he sounds like an Englishman. The Englishman he sounds like is Bertie Wooster. He also has Roy Jenkins's 'r' and Tony Benn's 's'. He talks about 'wepeat offendersh', and 'pointsh pweshently under conshiderwation'. It's all rather endearing. One imagines a Drones trip to the Gorbals, with a cocktail cabinet in the back of the charabanc.

Malicious English MPs began to ask questions about Scottish taxes, and in particular the subsidy Scotland receives from the rest of the UK. It turns out that, even taking North Sea oil into account, Scotland gets £7 billion more in public spending than it pays into the Exchequer in tax.

Now of course £7 billion may not seem a lot of money to you or me. It represents roughly the amount which has gone missing from the Treasury over the past few months. Who knows where that may be? Quite possibly in cyberspace, where cunning international firms

81

know where to hide it. Who would have thought, amidst all the futuristic jargon about the Information Super-Highway, that it would be clogged by unmarked white vans stuffed with used fifties?

However, £7 billion is quite a lot of money in Scotland, a region where only one-tenth of the United Kingdom's population actually lives. Mr Ian Bruce, the Conservative MP for Dorset South, asked disingenuously how much extra Scots would have to pay if they received the same funding from the Treasury for health and local government as the English do.

Mr Forsyth said that this would amount to £3.5 billion. Since each extra penny on Scottish income tax would raise only £130 million, 'it will be easy to work out how much extra tax would be needed'. (Another 27p in the pound, in fact, thought this does seem slightly improbable, since it would mean that some better-off Scots were paying more than two-thirds of their income in tax.)

You might imagine that all this munificence flowing from us to them would make some English politicians eager to give the Scots independence immediately, if only to get the accounts straight. Not at all. Mr Major cannot do enough to keep their love and respect. He even announced (having perfunctorily informed the Queen and the Dean and Chapter of Westminster, who actually own the thing) that the Stone of Destiny would be returned to Scotland. Some of us did not even know what the Stone of Destiny is, and vaguely assumed it must be some milky-white phosphorescent thing emitting deadly rays, as depicted in a Harrison Ford film, in which the evil Nazi holds it up while cackling, 'Yes. Ha! Ha! It is mine! Now I have absolute power and will rule the world!' It turned out to be the fancy name for the Stone of Scone. The Prime Minister announced its return home in a March-of-History tone of voice which reduced Labour MPs, English and Scottish, to unstoppable giggles.

However, the Scots in the Commons are rarely pleased with anything, and regard the time when England is doing its best to please them as the perfect occasion for getting angrier than ever.

Mr John Maxton, the Labour Member for Cathcart, denounced the blameless piece of rock as 'a feudal, mediaeval symbol of tyranny'. Mr Tommy Graham, the Labour MP for Renfrew West, suggested that the stone should be used for different political purposes. 'For every thousand unemployed people we should get a bagpiper and march the stone with two hundred unemployed bagpipers from one end of the country to another!'

Mr Major replied that unemployment was falling in Scotland. 'When we have that piper we will have people with new jobs, with permanent jobs, following that piper, instead of all those people who were only in work because of subsidies.'

A march of the employed, with pipers! Maybe they could march to Jarrow, and gloat at those without jobs. Still, it could have been worse. Mr Graham might have suggested two hundred pipers for every unemployed person.

Meanwhile, some of us are now convinced that full independence for Scotland is vital if we are to live peaceably together on this island. And if we have to paint blue stripes on our face to help achieve this, then we'd be happy to do so.

WILLIAM HAGUE:
The Young Pretender

He is like the star of an early science fiction film, The Man Who Aged Too Fast. *In his search for the elixir of youth, scientist Bill Hague makes a vital error in his calculations, and begins to grow old twice as fast as anyone else.*

Mr William Hague is quite the most terrifying figure in the Conservative government. So young, and yet so very, very old. He is famous for having electrified a Tory conference when he was sixteen years old, describing in a broad Yorkshire accent how, at a time when the summit of most young men's ambition is to find a girl who lets you put your hand in her blouse, he yearned only 'to roll back the frontiers of the state'.

Elderly then – one imagines his mother tucking him up in three-piece pyjamas – he has grown older at a frightening rate. He is now the youngest Cabinet Minister since Harold Wilson, who in appearance, accent and deportment he so much resembles. He is like the star of an early science fiction film, *The Man Who Aged Too Fast*. In his search for the elixir of youth, scientist Bill Hague makes a vital error in his calculations, and begins to grow old twice as fast as anyone else. The critics love it: 'Not bad' (*Daily Herald*); 'I've seen worse' (*Sunday Citizen*). Margaret Thatcher once compared him to Pitt the Younger, though I suspect that if they ever dug Pitt the Younger up, he would still look younger than Mr Hague.

Mr Hague is bald now, and his voice has the weary monotony of one who in his time has known all and seen all. By the time he is forty his remaining hairs will be white, and deep wrinkles will furrow his so briefly youthful face. When at the age of forty-one he becomes our youngest Prime Minister, he will hobble into Cabinet supported by young sprigs of sixty-five, making remarks like, 'In our day, pop songs had a tune. And you could hear the words.' One Tory MP suggested that he was so terminally untrendy 'he probably thinks that Tramps is a hostel for the homeless'.

What is most surprising is that Mr Hague has a secret vice. What he likes to do on Saturday mornings is to rise in his bachelor home, put a Meatloaf record on the turntable, and jump around, dancing and playing the air guitar. This makes him possibly the only Cabinet Minister to enjoy that particular hobby; one cannot, for example, picture Sir Patrick Mayhew sharing it. (Meatloaf's latest hit is entitled 'I'd Lie for You, and That's the Truth', which makes it a perfect politician's anthem.)

In the meantime he resembles your potential father-in-law, the good-natured fellow who is prepared to accept you, even to be friendly, provided he thinks your intentions are honourable.

His first appearance in the Commons as Secretary of State came when he was put in charge of Wales following the resignation of John Redwood. On his first day at the Dispatch Box, Welsh Labour, Liberal and Plaid Cymru MPs all boycotted Question Time on the grounds that they were fed up with having Englishmen who sit for English seats being put in charge of Wales.

Mr Hague handled it with avuncular jocularity. What he didn't do was make some absurdly complimentary remarks about his new fiefdom. Possibly at the school where they teach you to be extremely old, they hadn't told him how important this is, especially in Wales. The Welsh, like the Scots, are obsessed with the belief that the English have no time for them, and rarely concern themselves with Welsh culture, economy or general anxiety. In this they are perfectly correct. Therefore it is necessary for a new, English Welsh Secretary to make some remark along these lines: 'I would rather spend a wet weekend in Port Talbot than an entire month sunning myself on the beach in Barbados.' Nobody would believe you, but that's not the point. It's a form of grovelling, the more extreme the better; a way of saying, 'Look, I realise that if I am to rule you, I must offer you some form of obeisance.'

This can go horribly wrong. Mr John Redwood, Mr Hague's predecessor, once tried to sing along with the Welsh national anthem, in Welsh. Film of him with his mouth flapping silently up and down like a landed trout was often repeated on Welsh television. Mr Hague has been careful to learn the words. No doubt he could accompany himself on air guitar.

EDUCATION:
New Tricks for Old Dogmas

© Steve Bell 1995 ~ APOLOGIES TO LEWIS W. HINE

CONSERVATIVE POLICY ON EDUCATION

LABOUR POLICY ON EDUCATION

DR TATE'S PATENT SCHOOLROOM

Our Churchill which art in Nelson.
Hallowed be thy Rhodes. Thy Gradgrind come.
Thy Smiles be done in Kent as it is in Surrey.
Give us this day our Daily Mail,
And forgive us our Socialists, as we
forgive them that organise against us (Not!)
And lead us not into Trade Unionism,
but deliver us from Scargill.
For thine is the Jingo
the Land of Hope and Glory,
For ever and ever,
School without Roof
Amen.

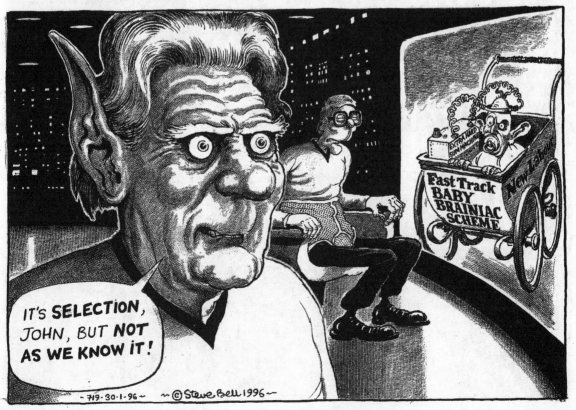

ROYALTY:
The Di is Cast

In a desperate attempt to proclaim their own loyalty to the House of Windsor, some writers have suggested that the failed marriages and the adultery prove that the Royals are people too, just like us. But we don't want them to be just like us.

Some of us (though not including Steve Bell) are firm believers in the Monarchy. It's a perfectly good system, in use around the world. Seven of the fifteen countries in the EU are Monarchies, and all but one are richer than us. Now and again someone whose idea of a good holiday read is a stack of Charter 88 discussion documents tells us that the Monarchy is the apex of the class system, and therefore the reason why Britain lags behind in every field of human endeavour except lager-drinking.

Nonsense. Do people in Japan point to the Emperor as the reason why they seem incapable of exporting cars and videos? Do Luxembourgers grumble that if they didn't have a Grand Duke they would not only be the richest people in Europe but the richest in the whole world? In Denmark the Queen rides around in a Buick convertible. She is much loved and the country makes a fortune exporting bacon, kitchenware and nubbly plastic play bricks. Spain's sudden transformation into a prosperous, successful and happy nation coincided with the return of the Monarchy.

And if we abolished the Monarchy, what on earth would we get in its place? Left-of-centre think tanks seem to imagine that we would

89

then be governed by a Parliament of Reason, ruling an egalitarian paradise in which no man doffs his cap and all work together for the common weal. In fact we would get a mess, devised in the interests of whoever formed the government of the day. And the very last people they would dream of consulting would be the left-of-centre think tanks who would still be churning out their pamphlets and staging modest demonstrations on College Green, complaining pitifully that they had spent years devising a new constitution. 'And so you have, so you have,' the politicians would sooth. 'Sadly, El Presidente Portillo has other ideas.'

But even if we agree to like a constitutional Monarchy (the system theoretically offers a focus for all the power in the realm while being powerless itself, thus forcing the great institutions such as the legislature, executive, armed forces, judiciary etc. to offer their fealty to a notion of the State rather than to each other. Of course it doesn't work out in practice. What system does?), do we have to have this lot? Why are we stuck with them? Do we have to tolerate the House of Windsor until the mob storms Buckingham Palace or Prince Charles demonstrates his famously sensitive nature and abdicates not just for himself but unto the thousandth generation?

These thoughts were prompted by the Queen's seventieth birthday, which turned out to be the occasion for a mass outpouring of slathering sycophancy by the Press. Possibly, at the back of their dim, pickled brains, the popular papers do feel just the faintest tremor of guilt about their treatment of the Royals. Conor Cruise O'Brien once

wrote that receiving the attentions of the British tabloids was like being picked up and shaken by some drunken hooligan who won't let go. Just once in every few years the yobbos feel they ought to be nice to the victim's dear old Mum.

Nor are the woes of the family entirely their own fault. Nobody could survive the relentless nature of the Press's attentions, the knowledge that nothing whatever in your private life is truly private, that even the people who make your bed might be noting the stains on the sheets.

But the Queen must take some blame. What is astonishing since she ascended the throne is not how much has changed, but how little. The Court still is a court in the old sense, filled with toadies jockeying and crawling for preferment. There are rival courts inside the family, too: an aide to Prince Charles once described how impossible it was for them to book the Royal Train, even a year ahead – the Queen's entourage always found a reason why it wouldn't be available.

His petty jealousies would have been appropriate in a fairy story about wicked queens and maltreated princesses. Early on in his marriage, he was supposed to be out working the streets on a visit to Germany, but went missing. He was found kicking a stone around the courtyard of the castle they were staying in, grumbling, 'They don't want to see me, they only want to see my wife.' In Australia we heard him say bitterly to the spectators lining the streets when she was on the opposite pavement, 'Well, you picked the wrong side of the street…'

Yes, the Queen has abolished some of the old protocol. At formal dinners she does not insist that everyone finishes eating when she does, and is happy to push a few last peas around the plate until informed that most people are through. This is unlike her sister, who even at house parties where she has invited herself, demands that everyone downs cutlery the moment she does, and refuses to permit anyone to go to bed before her. On the odd occasions I have seen Princess Margaret in action, I have been faintly shocked by the sight

"Orff with her ring" - AFTER TENNIEL - - ©Steve Bell 1995 -

707·22·12·95·

of distinguished elderly women curtseying to her as she stands there, as regal as anyone can be with a gin in one hand and a fag in the other.

Almost nothing obtrudes into the placidity of life at court. The Queen is surrounded by exactly the same kind of upper-class courtiers, with a gift for blending bossiness and servility in equal measure, who surrounded her ancestors and who surrounded her forty years ago. It seems inconceivable that she should ever appoint a black man, or a working-class woman. Her only real interest is horse racing, on which she spends some £400,000 a year.

She has a tremendous sense of duty, we are told. To be fair, in her obsession to be seen as regal, she has at least got the message; that we do not ask her to be a real, flesh-and-blood human being. Perhaps she was too busy reigning to give Prince Charles the attention a small boy needs – there's a famous picture of her being greeted by the tiny figure after she had made a massive Commonwealth trip, when she shook him by the hand.

In a desperate attempt to proclaim their loyalty to the House of Windsor, some writers have suggested that the failed marriages and the adultery prove that the Royals are people too, just like us. But we don't want them to be just like us, any more than the French want Marie France to have a string of toy boys, or the Americans would like the Statue of Liberty to go on holiday to have her toes sucked. All we ask is that they preserve some kind of dignity as national figureheads. If it's lovable venality we want, there's always Gillian Taylforth.

92

NICHOLAS SOAMES:
The Lard of the Manor

It is always a joy to see Mr Nicholas Soames, the Defence Minister, at the Dispatch Box. Mr Soames is that rarity among politicians, the man who says exactly the same thing in private as he does in public.

It is always a joy to see Mr Nicholas Soames, the Defence Minister, at the Dispatch Box. Mr Soames is that rarity among politicians, the man who says exactly the same thing in private as he does in public. There was a piece of upper-class slang which had a short vogue among plebeians a few years ago: hog-whimpering drunk. Mr Soames is hog-whimpering frank.

On one occasion, oh, many many moons before his marriage, I sat two places away from Mr Soames at a lunch. Between us was a beautiful young woman who I shall call Caroline. Mr Soames was animadverting on the state of the Conservative Party. 'Anyone who doesn't give John Major his full support is a nuclear-powered cunt,' he mused. Then, in a voice only a few decibels lower, he said to the young woman, 'Good God, you're absolutely gorgeous. Have I told you that I adore you, you beautiful creature?'

She giggled in a courteous kind of way. Then he returned to the topic of his own Party's shortcomings. 'My God, X is a complete and utter cunt, as I told him in the Smoking Room the other day. "X, you're a complete and utter cunt!" ' he roared, recreating the scene. Then, *sotto voce*, or what passes for *sotto voce* in Mr Soames's larynx, 'Why don't you sleep with me, Caroline? Everyone else sleeps with me. Why the hell won't you?'

Since Mr Soames's marriage, those days are gone, no doubt to the regret of many other lovely women, one of whom is alleged to have said that making love to him was like having a wardrobe fall on top of you with the key sticking out.

The topic of love is never far from Mr Soames's mind. For example, in his role as a Defence Minister, he was asked by Mrs Bridget Prentice about International Women's Week. In Mr Soames's past, every week was International Women's Week. The news that this fact was now officially celebrated brought something close to rapture to the Soames breast.

'I was not aware that this is International Women's Week,' he said, 'but a tremendous surge of pleasure comes over us when we hear the happy news, and we salute women everywhere!'

There were clearly limits to this delight, however. Another Labour MP asked whether the Ministry of Defence supported the cause of Opportunity 2000. Mr Soames appeared to have only the vaguest idea of what this might be. Since women in the British armed forces were promoted only on their merits, it sounded like politically correct nonsense to him.

This brought a great surge of pleasure to the Labour benches, since Opportunity 2000 was an initiative by the Conservative government, and so from Mr Soames's point of view, about as politically correct as it is possible to be.

Next Lady Olga Maitland surged to her feet. She mentioned that there were two female jet pilots in the Royal Air Force, and added, 'Are you aware of the important work being done in the field by women?'

This unintentional *double entendre* was too much for Mr Soames. It called up images of warm summer nights, of rosy-cheeked milkmaids concealed behind haystacks, a jug of cider to hand, saucy smiles dimpling soft cheeks.

'The great surge of women is beginning to be felt!' he cried, or rather gasped. In these circumstances, could the great surge of Soames be long delayed?

At last, and in the nick of time, a person of the male persuasion stood up. Mr Bernard Jenkin, the Tory MP for Colchester North, wanted to know the effect of some European Union directive on equality.

Mr Soames had time to collect himself. He is, after all, a Minister of the Crown. (Indeed, thanks to his friendship with Prince Charles, he will in the fullness of time minister to the Crown. It was Mr Soames who, on television, accused Princess Diana of being paranoid, and who was reproved by the Prime Minister the following day. This must have been rather like watching Captain Mainwaring from *Dad's Army* ticking off some wealthy subaltern in a Guards' regiment, the young man already the worse for several bumpers of Margaux. Technically Mr Major's rank is higher, but in every other way he would be regarded as an inferior.)

Mr Soames pondered Mr Jenkin's question. He is, after all, known to be a master of his brief. He contemplated; he replied. 'All that EC nonsense is way beyond me,' he bellowed, authoritatively.

The Labour benches, which had been worried – or possibly hoping – that Mr Soames would be the first person to die of a sexual frenzy at the Dispatch Box, collapsed with laughter. Betty Boothroyd said crisply, 'That remark closes the question down.'

But it didn't close Mr Soames down. His joke had created the most tremendous reaction. Like some mighty steam engine, he continued shaking with laughter. Just as you thought the flywheel must slow down, and the boiler stop wheezing, he began to shudder again, his vast pink face split by his gleeful smile. Ka-chunk, ka-chunk, kaaaaah-chunk, chunnnnk. Finally the whole frame slowed to a halt with only a few wisps of steam left where once a terrible explosion had threatened. There was one final heave of the shoulders as he turned round to grin at his friends, and the mighty Soames was stilled.

DANGER:
Spin Doctors at Work

American and British spin doctors work in very different ways. Americans tend to be rude, overbearing and demanding. Their British equivalents are much worse.

The term 'spin doctor' is, of course, American. It describes people employed by politicians and their parties to put a favourable 'spin' on political events and speeches. Why 'doctor' and not 'spin lawyer' or 'spin washerperson' I do not know.

American and British spin doctors work in very different ways. Americans tend to be rude, overbearing and demanding. Their British equivalents are much worse.

The phrase is tossed around in the Press and on television all the time these days, but most people aren't very clear about what these people (most are men, but an increasing number are women) actually do, or what the experience of being spun is like.

In America you encounter most of them during Presidential election campaigns. At a big debate between the candidates there will be literally dozens waiting in the hall, and their most important work is carried out in the twenty minutes or so after the debate has finished. Their task is to persuade the assembled media (who may

number hundreds or even thousands) that their man 'won' the debate. The most important spin doctors, the ones closest to the candidate himself, will brief the most important media: network political correspondents, the *New York Times*, the *Washington Post*, *Time*, *Newsweek* and so forth. If you represent the *Dogbreath, South Dakota*, or *Tribune-Bugle*, you may be lucky to have two minutes with a spotty nineteen-year-old youth whose name is unknown to the candidate himself. If you are a foreigner, you'll be lucky to get anyone at all.

This is how it goes:

Spin doctor: 'We're pleased, we're real pleased. Jim stuck to the playbook and he did great.'

Reporter: 'He did? What about the farming subsidies question, when he said the other guy's mother never married his father?'

Spin doctor: 'Yeah, wasn't that something? All our stats show that is going to play very big with single or divorced white women and incomes below twenty grand living on farms in key counties in Oklahoma – and Bill, you know how bad we need Oklahoma.'

Reporter: 'But hey, five minutes later he walked over to the other guy's podium and he spat right in his face. You're not going to tell us that was in the playbook? Jim just lost it, right?'

Spin doctor: 'Jeez, what can I say to you guys? Don't you listen? You're damn right it was in the playbook. Wait for the overnights from swing precincts in Peoria, and you'll see why it was in the goddamn playbook.'

Reporter: 'Jed, I gotta tell you. The part where he walked into the audience, grabbed two old ladies, held a gun to their heads and threatened to kill them unless he was elected President, well, our people are saying in an editorial tomorrow that this means he is unfit for office.'

Spin doctor: 'Your people! Huh, your people! Who in God's name in Washington reads the goddamn *Washington Post*? Nothing personal, Bill, but no one gives a flying fuck what the *Washington Post* says about squat. There's an electorate out there or maybe you didn't notice. And they loved it! I tell you, we're gonna clean that guy's clock!'('Cleaning someone's clock' is a favourite phrase in American political parlance. It derives from the ancient trade of clock cleaning, by way of boxing, and means to dismantle something totally, leaving the working parts all over the bench. Corporate and political slang in America is often concerned with making ordinary, workaday activities sound as if they were part of some mighty physical struggle, thus 'We're gonna wrestle him to the mat' generally means 'Suggest a possible alternative approach to the problem' and 'Kick ass' implies 'Send a peevish memo'.)

In Britain, before spin doctors were called spin doctors, they were known as Press Secretaries. They preferred murmurs to shouts. For example, Sir Tom McCaffrey was Press Secretary to Jim Callaghan when he was Prime Minister. Sir Tom would no more have yelled or sworn at someone than he would have consulted the intestines of eviscerated crows before briefing the Parliamentary Lobby.

For instance, if your paper had written an article headlined

'Labour Plans Slaughter of the First-Born' and commencing, 'Prime Minister Jim Callaghan has proposed a new bill to allow the execution of all first-born children as a means of economising on child benefit payments,' Tom would come up to you later in the day and murmur something along the lines of: 'Prime Minister a little puzzled by your piece this morning… tells me he has no idea where it came from… wonders whether you might possibly have confused it with the scheme to slaughter diseased ducks in the High Wycombe area…' But he would never get cross.

All this changed with the arrival of Bernard (now Sir Bernard) Ingham, a former Labour candidate and *Guardian* reporter, who was the first real British spin doctor, in the sense that he saw his job as changing the news to suit his employer rather than merely trying to put the best gloss he could on events. He was the right man at the right time, because Mrs Thatcher had a problem. Being Margaret Thatcher all day was a terrible strain. No one could manage it. It would be like asking a Shakespearean actor to be Richard III not just for the course of the play but for twenty-four hours. So she employed Bernard to be Mrs Thatcher when she was too tired and too busy.

It was not always so. Once when Bernard was Press Secretary to Tony Benn, I phoned him to ask why the then Energy Secretary had made a rather curious speech. The following (genuine) conversation took place, and you will quickly see why I have broken a promise made in the course of it:

Me: 'Why do you think Tony Benn said that?'

Bernard: 'I do know, and I'll tell you, but you have to promise never, ever, to say it was me.'

Me (by now quite excited about a potential scoop): 'Yes, of course I'll promise.'

Bernard: 'I've got a kid, you know, and a mortgage. If it ever gets out that I told you, I'll lose my job.'

Me: 'I promise I'll never breathe a word, not to anyone.'

Bernard: 'Right then, so I've got your word.'

Me: 'Yes, yes!'

Bernard: 'The reason is that the Secretary of State is stark, staring mad.'

Years later he went to work for Mrs Thatcher. Bernard was a classic example of the spin doctor in that he knew better than his own boss what his boss was thinking. This could lead to embarrassment and difficulty, as when he told lobby journalists that it didn't matter whether the pound sterling fell to parity with the dollar. Of course, in the ideal, Platonic Thatcherite world it wouldn't matter if the pound fell to five cents against the dollar: the market knows all, sees all, decrees all, and there is less point in trying to tamper with it than with the weather. Still, what Bernard hadn't taken into account was the fact that the market does not share this view of its own omniscience, and was inclined to believe that if the Prime Minister's Press Secretary was happy for the pound to decline, then perhaps they ought to bring it down on his behalf.

Much of the time Bernard was Mrs Thatcher. By becoming a sort of holographic image of the Prime Minister his words gained a conviction which the old murmurers could never have managed. During the Falklands War you could almost see the salt spray on his face as he stood on the bridge of *HMS Invincible,* plunging through the grey waters of the south Atlantic. Here is a genuine exchange from those days:

Me: 'Is the Prime Minister aware that there are some Tory back-benchers who have serious doubts about her strategy?'

Bernard: 'So, it's true what they say. She is the only man among the lot of them.'

(Later.) Reporter sympathetic to Mrs Thatcher: 'Has the Prime Minister seen the quite disgusting pictures of General Galtieri, on the Falkland Islands, eating a penguin?'

Reporter on another paper (waking up from a deep, untroubled sleep): 'Wha'? Wha'? Nothing wrong with that. Fellow probably likes a chocolate biscuit with his morning coffee.'

Bernard has no greater admirer than Mr Alastair Campbell, who is Tony Blair's Press Secretary. Mr Campbell used to be a political reporter, in the sense that he would write intensely admiring articles about the people he admired intensely. One was Mr Neil Kinnock. He was also a considerable admirer of the late Robert Maxwell. There was a celebrated incident on the day in 1992 when Mr Maxwell was first reported missing from his yacht.

My colleague on the *Guardian,* Michael White, sauntered towards the *Daily Mirror* room in the Commons press gallery, mistakenly assuming that Mr Maxwell's employees would share his view that he was dead, and would share his satisfaction at this event. On his short journey to the *Mirror* staff, he picked up a joke, which he (mistakenly) thought might amuse them, and asked, 'Have you heard the one about Cap'n Bob-bob-bob...?'

Instead of chuckling, Mr Campbell hit him. Mr White hit him back, drawing blood. Ringside judges would have had to award the bout to White who is, however, generous to his opponent, pointing out that his own remark had been tasteless in the extreme and that many employees of the *Daily Mirror* must have been anxious about their future that day. However, I prefer to recall that Mr Campbell was the man who hit a colleague for being rude about Robert Maxwell.

Modern spin doctors do not believe in the muttered reproof over a friendly drink. They prefer the bellowed assault down the phone. Editors are called as they prepare their children for the school run. Those who have written a front-page article deemed unhelpful to the Labour cause (or more particularly, the Leader's cause, since the Party is as full of rival factions as any mediaeval court) are liable to be telephoned at 1.00 in the morning and harangued, loudly. 'Call that journalism? That's effing crap, that's not journalism... '

On a trip to the United States, Mr Campbell took issue with Robert Peston, the political editor of the *Financial Times.* As is customary, during the long flight out, the Party leader had invited a handful of journalists to chat to him. As is also customary, the privileged reporters were expected to share the *pensées* and *aperçus*

they received with their colleagues. Mr Blair had been discussing the
point at which increased taxes would apply to people on higher
earnings, and something he said led Mr Peston to believe that those
receiving up to £40,000 a year at least would not have to pay any
more. This, it transpired, was not the view Mr Blair wished to
communicate, but by the time he realised what was happening, Mr
Peston had shared the information with the other hacks at the back
of the plane.

From that moment on, Mr Peston's life was turned into an earthly
Vale of Tears. Mr Campbell harangued him in the most extreme
language both to his face, and to his colleagues behind his back.
Whereas Sir Tom McCaffrey might have spoken about 'A difference
of emphasis, I fear,' Mr Campbell said, 'Here's Peston, spinning for
the Tories again!' or, more simply, 'Cunt!' He kept this up for some
time, pursuing Mr Peston around the great cities of the eastern
seaboard.

Now Mr Peston is a grown man, and can look after himself –
though there are few advantages to being an enemy of Mr Campbell,
who uses his considerable knowledge as a means of rewarding those
who please him and punishing those who don't. The curious thing is
that the *Financial Times* has a greater regard for the facts than any
other. (They have to; money is riding on their reports. If the *Telegraph*
gets it wrong, blood pressure rises. If the *FT* gets it wrong, the Stock
Exchange falls.) The *FT* is also one of the few newspapers to have
supported Labour in the 1992 election. And to cap it all, Mr Peston's

father is actually a front-bench spokesman in the House of Lords –
for the Labour Party.

But in the new hard, masculine world of spin, such considerations
mean nothing. On foreign trips, it is sometimes Mr Campbell's
practice to receive accounts of the visit in the British newspapers, sent
from London by fax. He will then hand these out to their authors,
often with a word of praise or a shout of admonition. 'This is crap,' or
'Crap headline, not a bad story,' or, to one reporter (who his
colleagues believe had merely rewritten a Labour Party press release),
'Excellent!' On another occasion, Mr Campbell was briefing a lobby
correspondent about a speech Mr Blair was about to make. The
reporter expressed puzzlement about one paragraph. The silver-
tongued amanuensis glowered at him and shouted, 'Just shut up, and
write it down!'

On the occasion that Tony Blair came out against the London tube
strike, he told a reporter on the *Evening Standard*, 'And if you call it a
U-turn, I'll take your head off.'

Mr Campbell's close associate (and great rival) is Peter
Mandelson, now the MP for Hartlepool. When Tony Blair had a
great success in his first Party Conference speech, delivered in the
autumn of 1994, Mr Campbell and Mr Mandelson began a
competitive tantrum about who had contributed most to the text of
the speech. Strangest of all, they held this tantrum in public, through
the medium of Mr Campbell's newspaper column.

If Mr Mandelson likes you, he treats you with all the joyful
loyalty of William Brown's dog Jumble. If he doesn't, he regards you
with loathing and contempt. Being the recipient of his affection and
admiration must be like being gummed by a toothless Rottweiler.

Those who offend him are boycotted, though usually for a set
period of time. Like community service, it is a relatively painless
means of teaching people the error of their ways. One lobby
correspondent deemed to have behaved badly was informed that he
would be ignored for the next three weeks. At a party during the
1994 Labour conference I was in conversation with James Naughtie
of the *Today* programme and Mr Barry Cox, a television executive
who had helped to finance Mr Blair's leadership campaign. These
were clearly persons of some consequence in Mr Mandelson's life,
which is perhaps why I felt a frisson of admiration when he marched
up to Mr Naughtie, abruptly interrupted our conversation, and
announced, 'I have a bone to pick with you' – while grabbing him by
the lapels. (Luckily Mr Naughtie forgave him, and later that year
invited him to a party at his home where
he grabbed me by the lapels for some
other error, real or imagined.)

For a grey eminence, supposedly
gliding through the shadows, flitting
here and there, gently inserting a word in
this person's ear, dropping a dribble of
poison into another, Mr Mandelson gets
into the newspapers an awful lot. Hardly
a weekend goes by without another
three-page profile in one of the Saturday

I'M YOUR NEW
SPIN DOCTOR

magazines, or a thundering denunciation in a Monday leader article. Should Mr Mandelson murmur confidentially to a trusted correspondent that Mr Gordon Brown's influence in the higher reaches of the Labour leadership is on the wane, then the very next day an excitable article will proclaim that the two men are at daggers drawn. They are a little like those couples in offices who are having an adulterous affair; they would like to think their secret is safe, yet rather enjoy the fact that every detail is followed with salacious satisfaction by the rest of the staff. In Labour politics, a good loathing is every bit as gratifying to the onlookers as sex would be in the real world outside.

And yet Mr Mandelson does have a certain fascinating charm. Now a member of his Party's front bench, he makes only rare spoken interventions (words spoken in the Commons Chamber suffer from the drawback of being on the record) but may frequently be seen slumped on the green benches, legs slightly apart, arms across his chest, eyes hooded like a lizard after a good lunch. Now and again he consults a silent beeper, which has no doubt alerted him to a message by vibrating gently against his thigh. The implication is plain: the charade in front of me is of little moment. All truly important activity is taking place outside here, and I am in constant electronic touch with it.

At the 1995 Labour conference, Steve Bell and I were standing just below the platform, to one side. Bell remarked that he had not yet seen Mandelson. Was he present? I said I was certain that he was, but probably hiding behind the scenes. At that very moment a curtain to one side of the stage fluttered aside and out stepped Mandelson. Bell raised his camcorder to film him, and I expected this most secretive of spin doctors to spin round and disappear once more. But he didn't. Instead he smiled and – the only word for it – *sashayed* towards us, pirouetting as he came, preening himself on his toes, smiling self-consciously for the cameras, for all the world as if he were being filmed by friends on a Costa Brava beach. It was a touching, even sweet moment, in the life of our leading Sultan of Spin.

Another difference between the spin doctors of today and the Press Secretaries of the past is the loss of irony. The old-fashioned spokesmen never tried to pretend that they were dealing with objective fact. Their tone implied a conspiratorial relationship with the Press: we know that at least half of what we say is nonsense; you know it too, and we are only pretending to fool each other.

Modern spin doctors, however, need to believe that everything they say is true. For this reason they tend to address journalists, even over a private drink, as if they were at a public meeting. 'You'll have noticed the contemptible decision of the Tory government…, ' they will say. Or 'Once again, our polls show there is massive public support for the stand Tony is taking… ' or 'I hardly need to point out to you how Portillo's position is the exact opposite of the one he claimed to have last year…' – even when they are speaking to people they know are not even Labour supporters. This gives their conversation a strange, disjointed air, as if one was not talking to a human being, but watching a party political broadcast on TV. If you try to speak to them as if they were physically present, corporeal persons, a blank look comes into their eyes and they begin to riffle through a folder of statistics.

A spin doctor never gives up. One of their most important skills is to be so determined, so persistent, and so incredibly boring that the journalist gives in for a quiet life. 'My man is making a fascinating new speech on new trends in national insurance,' he tells you. 'Oh,' you reply, 'I'm afraid it's rather a busy night, what with several members of the Royal Family having been killed in a helicopter crash.'

A few moments later he's back. 'I've been talking to the *Telegraph* and the *Indy,* and they are very excited about these new proposals on national insurance. In fact, I'd not be a bit surprised if they didn't make them the lead story.'

You reply that this seems highly unlikely, given the story about the dead Royals. He makes a small concession: 'Well, maybe so, but it will be the second lead, for sure. I'm only telling you so that you don't look stupid when the first editions come out tonight.'

By this stage you are ready to throw things. But he has still not given up. Half an hour later, he's back, rubbing his hands. 'The other lot are really getting upset about those national insurance proposals! Reading between the lines of their hand-out, they seem to be saying our policy could lose them the next election! I just thought I'd mention it. It's the kind of thing your paper is keen on, and I know you need a good story...' In the end they may well be lucky. A small story of a few paragraphs appears, labelled 'New Insurance Row Storm'; the spin doctor's boss is happy, the spin doctor is delighted, and the readers are bored out of their minds.

Spin doctors can be bullied back. On one occasion we in the *Guardian* office at the Commons had been nagged interminably about the paper's decision to give prominence to a speech by John Major rather than one made the same night by Tony Blair. A succession of Labour spin doctors appeared, wheedling and moaning about the paper's choice, deploying a blend of sycophancy and sarcasm. Finally when one egregiously whinging junior appeared, Michael White's patience snapped.

'I'll tell you why we didn't lead the paper on Blair's speech,' he said. 'We didn't lead it on Blair's speech because, thanks to you and your colleagues, this story was trailed in *The Times* yesterday, and what's more when he made the speech there was very little in it that was very new or interesting, and may I remind you that for all his faults, John Major is still the Prime Minister of this country, unlike Tony Blair, even if he seems to give the impression sometimes that he has already got the job...' And more of the same.

The spin para-medic reeled back in confusion. 'I didn't realise you would take it seriously,' he stammered.

'I'm not taking it seriously,' said White. 'If I had taken what you said seriously, you would have been pitched through that window ten minutes ago. Now get out!' But was he back the next day? Of course. Just as ambitious boxers have to roll with the blows, spin doctors have whiplash with the spin.

Me Hezza, You John

Parliament still has some fine spectacles to offer us, and Heseltine versus Prescott is one.

Parliament still has some fine spectacles to offer us, and Heseltine versus Prescott is one. Back in 1995, Mr Heseltine was made Deputy Prime Minister and First Secretary of State, titles as magnificent as they are meaningless. The origins of this splendour are somewhat obscure. It is known that, on the morning of the leadership election in July, the Whips had warned that Mr Major's position was perilous. The Prime Minister might well defeat the challenger, John Redwood, but the margin of victory could be so narrow that his position would be undermined for the rest of his days in office.

That morning Mr Heseltine spent several hours in Downing Street. In the afternoon his supporters trooped into the committee room to vote for Mr Major, and made a point of ostentatiously showing their colleagues where they had placed the cross. Mr Major won fairly comfortably, his associates declared a mighty victory, and the next day Mr Heseltine's appointment as Lord High Everything Else was announced.

There was much speculation. Some claimed that matters were as

they appeared at first sight. Mr Heseltine had realised that if John Redwood did well enough to bring about the Prime Minister's resignation, then he, not Heseltine, would reap the harvest. He had therefore guaranteed Mr Major's victory and his own advancement at the same time. He had stayed such a long time in Downing Street because it had taken him several hours to find an office grand enough for his purposes.

Others argued that this was naïve. Mr Heseltine, they say, never gives up, ever. He must have reached some kind of arrangement with Mr Major – that Major would step down at some time or for some reason. But the fifth anniversary of his assuming the premiership passed; the local government elections were disastrous, as they always are, and yet Mr Major was still there. Was it the end? Had we reached the elegiac conclusion to Mr Heseltine's political life? (One imagines him played by Donald Wolfit. I know that Wolfit is dead, but these days, with computer animation, that is a very minor problem.)

Now he is fated to face Mr Prescott, during the monthly Deputy Prime Minister's Question Time, and whenever Mr Major is away for the main event. Frequently he accuses Mr Prescott of being in the grip of spin doctors, or rather, one spin doctor – Mr Peter Mandelson, who is the Cardinal Richelieu of the present Labour leadership.

There is a particularly piquant pleasure here for Mr Heseltine since, like everyone else, he knows that for years Mr Prescott loathed

and detested Mr Mandelson and all those who think and act like him. 'The pretty people,' he used to call them scornfully. This is even more delightful coming from Mr Heseltine who is himself the apotheosis of all gyratory physicians: the Sultan of Swirl, the Maestro of Maelstrom, a man who could turn the bagel of fact into the Möbius strip of propaganda.

One extraordinary, and little-known, fact is that Hezza's monumental hair is thinning. This news, as full of omens and portents as the disappearance of the ravens from the Tower or the departure of the apes from Gibraltar would be, came from a Tory MP who had sat behind him. Mr Heseltine is beginning to suffer from crown baldness, and it is only the majestic backward sweep of his remaining tresses which keeps him from becoming the highest placed slaphead in the country.

I don't know why people say they can't understand John Prescott. I always understand him perfectly. Perhaps it is because we both come from Hull. In wintertime, when the foggy dark comes early and the lights swing perilously from the market stalls, the traders there sell gimcrack rubbish at unbeatable prices. It is a metaphor for the House of Commons.

'Not only am I gonna sell you this beautiful thirty-six-piece dinner service, I'm going to throw in this gorgeous canteen of cutlery, it's reely luvvly, ent'it, darling, and this gravy boat, luke at that craftsmanship, and am I gonna charge you a tenner, noh I am not, am I gonna ask you fer nine quid, no way, tell yer what, I dunno what's the marrer wi' me, this is what ah'll give you on top of all this.'

Like Mr Prescott they had more things to say than the time available to say them. The words tumbled over each other like unruly children running indoors. Whole words and clauses, entire sentences are lost in the headlong rush to close the sale. But everyone listening knows precisely what is meant.

This is the difference between Mr Prescott and, say, John Major. Mr Major speaks in clear, largely grammatical sentences. But you can puzzle for hours to work out what he really means.

Mr Prescott gave a bravura performance on his stall at the end of the Budget debate. The thoughts came one after the other in short, tightly bound clusters, like the electronic pulses which feed a computer. We were bowling along down Mr Prescott's Opinion Super-Highway, with no cones or speed limits to slow us down.

On private financing: 'We were talking about this Dispatch Box when they said we couldn't have!' Would Labour raise taxes? 'We will make the appropriate decision at the level of time!'

What lessons can we learn from more prosperous nations? 'Any visit to these countries knows it is much as much public investment as private investment.' Or on a different matter, whose topic now escapes me, 'That has always been our case, always the problem we address ourselves to.'

Long words are reduced to a few syllables to save precious time: 'Competness… devalation.' Then at the end of the speech, this ringing new slogan: 'It's not just how much you spend, but how much you spend!'

I don't want to be condescending to Mr Prescott. The audience knew what he meant and they probably half-believed it, like the crowds at the market stall who are tempted, even if they know the pattern will rub off the gravy boat after three washes.

And Mr Heseltine was worse. His speech too was a farrago of dubious statistics and implausible claims, though he does do a slightly more upmarket patter. 'Lissen, look at this Sèvres ware. Smashing stuff, darling. Am I gonna charge you ten grand? Nah. I'm not even gonna charge you eight grand. All I want is a miserable five thousand nicker and I'll throw in this gorgeous Meissen fondue set!'

That day one of the newspapers had published a poem, a piece of doggerel by one Fleur Adcock, who claimed to have a passion for Mr Prescott. Mr Heseltine quoted it at length: 'In the dream I was kissing John Prescott. We were leaning avidly forward, certain protruberances under our clothing, brushing each other's fronts.'

Those of us whose principal protuberance is our stomach would normally be grateful for such yearning. Mr Prescott, however, looked deeply pained, perhaps because his wife was watching from the Gallery.

ANOTHER FINE MESS!

© Steve Bell 1994 — 492. 14·9·94

Kenneth Clarke and Gordon Brown are on the way to becoming one of the nation's best-loved double acts. Like Laurel and Hardy, they are entirely distinct characters, yet the comic chemistry between them seems to work, somehow.

Kenneth Clarke and Gordon Brown are on the way to becoming one of the nation's best-loved double acts. Like Laurel and Hardy, they are entirely distinct characters, yet the comic chemistry between them seems to work, somehow. Because they are so different they don't see a great deal of each other when they are not together on stage or rehearsing one of their popular routines. Interviews in fan magazines hint at a mutual dislike ('We find we see enough of each other professionally; when the lights go down, we go straight home to our families.' We ask ourselves, is it that their wives do not get on? Is it true, as the rumours say, that they detest each other, and off-stage communicate only through their agent?)

Ken likes to relax and enjoy himself. He tends to hurry though his speeches like a man who has just realised that it's almost closing time and the nearest pub is ten minutes' walk. He actually bellies up to the Dispatch Box, and leans on it with his elbow to one side, like a regular waiting for his mug to be taken off its hook and filled brimming with ale by the Speaker. (She plays the part. Betty

Boothroyd's voice is refined Northern for most of the time – rather like Annie Walker's, as older viewers of *Coronation Street* will remember. When she gets angry, her voice goes up an octave or so and gradually becomes broad Yorkshire. You expect her to shout, 'If ah don't have a bit of 'ush, ah shall put towels back on taps!')

An American Cabinet Member was once forced to resign for making a racist joke in which he claimed that all black men wanted was 'loose shoes, tight pussy and a warm place to shit'. Mr Clarke's sexual mores are no doubt beyond criticism, but his pleasure in the first of these privileges somehow leads one's mind on to the others. Loose shoes, tight monetary policy and a warm pasty to eat, perhaps.

As a youth he was a train-spotter, though of a rather superior kind, going on long charabanc trips to locomotive sheds rather than standing at the end of the platform at Crewe. Now he is a bird-watcher. His wife likes ancient buildings. Their ideal holiday would consist of wading across a salt marsh towards a Romanesque cathedral.

When he's not doing that, he enjoys sport. If you put him in a room with the Governor of the Bank of England in one corner, John Maynard Keynes in another and Adam Smith in the third, he'd watch the football match on the TV in the fourth. If they ever get round to doing an edition of *Loaded* magazine for middle-aged men ('Jiggy-jig in Pall Mall: where to have it off in London's Clubland' and 'Kathy Kirby as you've never seen her before') he would be a guest editor.

110

ST GORDON REASSURING THE DRAGON

© Steve Bell 1996

Gordon Brown is, by contrast, an obsessive worker. He sits at his computer, by his fax, with his mobile phone, fiddling with his e:mail. What he likes doing is phoning journalists with some horror story about Conservative profligacy which he has number crunched on his brand new Japanese number cruncher. Some of these appalling stories are true, others not so true, and many are irrelevant to anything. But the discovery of each one makes Mr Brown as happy as the sight of a golden eagle on his raspberry canes would make Mr Clarke. Recently Sue Lawley caused some annoyance by enquiring of Mr Brown, on *Desert Island Discs,* whether he was gay. Of course he isn't gay; he hasn't got the time.

When the two face each other across the Dispatch Box, they increasingly resemble two grumpy old men in a pub. It's their act. What makes it funny, apart from Mr Clarke's trademark gesture of hitching up his trousers to emphasise a point, is the way they allow the pointless and the irrelevant to take them to new heights of obsessiveness.

The two old men chunter on, nominally addressing each other, in fact barely communicating. Gordon Brown alleges that we are slipping down something called the World Prosperity League, which bears as much relation to reality as the Fantasy Football charts.

They throw disjointed, mismatched statistics at each other. 'Largest fall in unemployment of any major European country… shameful record of investment… longest hours worked in any G7 economy… exports booming as never before… manufacturing output

ONE OLD LADY AND SOPHISTICATED FINANCIAL INSTRUMENT SUPPORT

UNEMPLOYMENT FIGURES

lower than at any time since the Peasants' Revolt… 5.7 per cent!… 2.8 billion!…18 points!… four times as much as four years ago!'

Now and again they pause in this endless, fruitless exchange to refresh their glasses. 'Another pint of Todger and a packet of scratchings, please Ted, and I suppose you'd better ask that miserable bugger in the corner what he wants.'

It is possible that one day their roles will be reversed, at least until the Conservative Party sorts itself out. Mr Brown will stand to the Speaker's right, and Mr Clarke to her left. But it will be hard for the rest of us to detect any difference. Mr Brown will continue to be morose, Mr Clarke cheerful; they will merely have a new set of meaningless statistics to mutter at each other.

YOUR COUNTRY

NEEDS YOU

It's as if one's dog had died

112

THERE'S NOT ENOUGH SLACK IN THE ECONOMY

HELP INFLATION; HELP THE FAT MAN; LOSE YOUR JOB TODAY

114

RAIL PRIVATISATION:
Diddly and Dumber

The first privatised train I took turned out to be identical to a British Rail train, in the same livery, operated by the same staff and carrying the same surly youths with their feet up on the seat. It was even the same twelve minutes late.

I live on a privatised railway line, and it's been instructive to be smeared on to a microscope slide in the great laboratory of Thatcherite natural philosophy. One of the things that happens quite often is that there is a points or signal failure somewhere along the line into London. In the evil, misbegotten, fuddy-duddy days of the dinosaur British Rail, a couple of blokes in orange vests would have wandered out on to the line and fixed it straight away, causing perhaps ten minutes' delay to commuters.

Now the task must be undertaken instead by men specially dispatched from the nearest Railtrack depot, which is ten miles away in the wrong direction. This means – and you have to admire the peculiarly British genius behind this plan – that the crew have to drive by road through rush-hour traffic which has been made worse by the fact that the repairs they are going to carry out have not yet been carried out. This leads to chaos, during which tens of thousands of people are held up for two or even three hours.

I would say that the government is being Pollyannaish over rail privatisation, except that in Eleanor H. Porter's admirable novel

115

about that young lady it turns out that, by playing 'The Glad Game', she turns out to be the only realist in a town full of pessimists and misanthropes. This cannot be said of our government, which ignores every shred of real information which might conflict with its own demented optimism.

The first privatised train I took turned out to be identical to a British Rail train, in the same livery, operated by the same staff and carrying the same surly youths with their feet up on the seat. It was even the same twelve minutes late. These days nostalgia is just another source of instant gratification.

Still, I was fortunate. On the same line the previous day I would have travelled with the Transport Secretary, Sir George Young, and Mr Toby Jessell, who will shortly be my MP. The two men had risen at 4.30 a.m. to ride the very first privatised train in the country. 'You must be mad!' someone shouted at him, across the House. 'Perhaps I am mad,' he admitted, and a few of his colleagues could be seen nodding, almost imperceptibly.

'The train was clean and punctual, so my constituents can now look forward to an improved service!' (You pillock, one wanted to shout, of course they made sure that with VIPs travelling, it was clean and punctual. What did he imagine? That the management would say, 'Look, lads, we've got to be straight about this. We must make sure that Sir George – our Thin Controller – gets precisely the experience that a typical traveller would get. So let's scatter a few Tango cans around the carriage, and keep it in the sidings until it's

117

twenty minutes late'?)

'It was a particular pleasure to meet my hon friend at 5.00 on Twickenham station,' said Sir George, straining credulity further than most of us would dare. 'He was able to point out certain interesting features on our way to Waterloo.'

As it happens, you cannot point out many interesting features at 5.15 on a February morning, since it is pitch dark. Perhaps Mr Jessell, an enthusiastic, Tiggerish sort of fellow, simply pointed to where they were. 'That's where Oddbins is, Secretary of State, there's Look-In Video Rental, and ah yes, Mr Frisby the butcher! His loin chops are very popular around here!'

'Fascinating, Toby, quite fascinating,' Sir George would murmur in his courteous way, perhaps wondering if there was a restaurant car he could escape to. At this point the guard would come on the intercom to explain why the train had stopped.

Sir George had the embarrassment, on the second day of privatisation, of learning that one of the new companies had been banned from taking over after it had been discovered that they were fiddling the takings. They had been making it appear that passengers buying through tickets had spent a greater proportion of their journey on the company's tracks. Labour MPs affected horror and astonishment at this, though I don't see why; a certain element of sleaze and creative bookkeeping cuisine clings to almost all this government's enterprises.

Why, it was probably in their prospectus, already couched in the kind of demented corporate jargon in which all modern enterprises are conducted: 'We propose to construct an aggressive on-going reciprocal programme of creative revenue enhancement…'

Mr Nigel Spearing said that he had asked the new company to stop trains in his own constituency of West Ham. This seemed reasonable, since West Ham is on the way and passengers would be able to change there for two tube lines and another railway. 'They refused, claiming that they would lose revenue from there to Fenchurch Street,' he said.

Not stopping trains because the passengers would only take advantage, and get off!

Perhaps the company which buys the East Coast line will copy this idea and refuse to stop at York, obliging everyone to pay the full fare to go to Edinburgh.

RAILTHEFT

119

THE FAT CAT FLAP

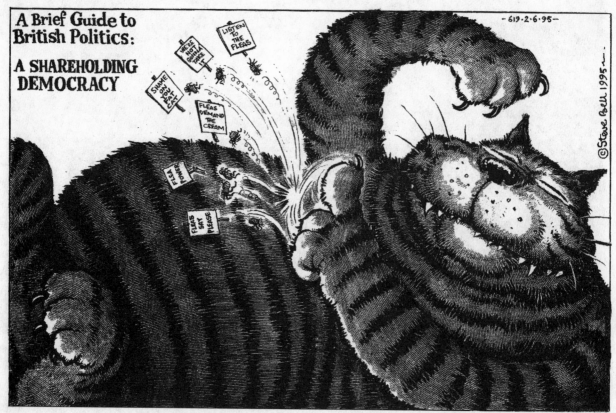

A Brief Guide to
British Politics:

A SHAREHOLDING
DEMOCRACY

IT'S A DEAL!! I KEEP THE ELEPHANT AND YOU KEEP THE CRAP!

BRITISH ENERGY

— 732 · 22·2·96 —

© Steve Bell 1996

122

Does my Right Honourable Friend Not Agree?

What keeps the wheels of British political life turning? Is it money? Or power? Influence and patronage? All these are important but perhaps none of them is as crucial as grease. Grease has become central to the political process. It is a currency, like tobacco in prisons. Or rather, it is part of a formalised ritual, whose precise meaning is lost in time, yet which still helps to maintain the governing class in power.

The way that grease is used to indicate social status could be studied, in the way that naturalists observe baboons pointing their blue bottoms at more important baboons, or anthropologists trace patterns of authority in Pacific islands. To us, in the West, it seems peculiar, irrational, even heathen. One can imagine how a visiting sociologist from America or Europe might describe it:

'According to age-old tradition in the British Isles, when a man or woman reaches a certain position in government, it is incumbent on those lower in the pecking order to offer him obsequious compliments in public. This ritual takes place during certain fixed periods, known as "Question Time". The "questions" have little or no meaning – indeed, for the most part they are untrue, being the incantation of an ancient, unvarying form of words. However, they serve their ceremonial purpose by indicating the comparatively high standing of the recipient, who must reply with a traditional acknowledgement of the grease which has been offered. The correct form of words is either "I am grateful to my honourable friend…" or else "I agree wholeheartedly with my honourable friend…"

'Being obliged to ask grovelling and misleading questions is a form of symbolic self-abasement by the "back-bencher", as he is known to the tribe. Yet, paradoxically – and bizarrely to our more rational Western minds – this is also designed to allow the greaser to become one of the tribal elders himself. Through the ritual of kowtowing, the greaser indicates that he accepts the authority of the "government" and will do nothing to challenge its power or prestige, provided he is permitted to join at a later date. After innumerable performances of this ceremony, many "back-benchers" will indeed be promoted, and as they themselves climb the ladder of power, others will be encouraged in turn to flatter them. In this way, the status quo is constantly re-established and reinforced. So-called "rogue" back-benchers, who choose not to humiliate themselves in this fashion, can be kept outside the inner circle, where they are prevented from challenging the structure of power and the belief system which sustains the government. Oddly enough, these people do not live in grass huts or have bones through their noses, but because of their ignorance of other cultures, they imagine themselves to be living in one of the world's most advanced civilisations.'

What keeps the wheels of British political life turning? Is it money? Or power? Influence and patronage? All these are important but perhaps none of them is as crucial as grease. Grease has become central to the political process. It is a currency, like tobacco in prisons.

In the past, back-bench MPs were supposed to act as a brake on the executive. They were watchdogs, in theory at least, ready to bark whenever government came creeping round the back to steal our freedoms or our money. Many of them held ministerial preferment in contempt. They were prepared to be loyal to their Party, in the same way that they had been loyal to their regiments, but the notion that this meant public obeisance to the more senior officers would have appalled them. They would have been equally horrified by the idea that translation to the higher ranks involved grovelling to the members of the promotions board.

Now for the most part, government back-benchers are toadies and apple-polishers. But even cringing and truckling are beyond them if they don't have help. Frequently they are given a sheet of supplementary questions to ask, lists of 'facts' which can be tacked on to any reply. For instance, question thirteen might be 'To ask the Secretary of State what plans the government has for the future of the British beer-mat industry'.

The Minister stands up and says that beer-mat production is up by seventy-five per cent over the past fifteen years, and that the government's firm resolve not to accept the Social Chapter of the Maastricht Treaty means that the future for beer-mats looks even brighter. Up stands the young lickspittle to read out the supplementary. (Or rather, not to read it out, since the ritual insists that this is not allowed. Instead he commits as much of it as he can to memory, then regurgitates it, like a mother bird sicking up a chewed worm into her nestlings' beaks.) 'Does my right honourable friend not agree that the beer-mat makers of Britain, many of whom live in my constituency, are unanimously grateful for this government's wise policies which have increased their prosperity and made their jobs more secure, and that if the Party opposite ever came into power, the imposition of a minimum wage could add hugely to the costs of beer-mat manufacture and allow cheap Taiwanese beer-mats to flood into the British market...'

This may seem horribly long-winded, but that's because it is. The fake questions offered to the bootlickers are crammed with 'facts', and the arcane details of the ritual demand that as many of these are produced as possible. Each additional 'fact' scores extra points with the Whips, rather in the way that the Grand Vizier to a particularly insecure Emperor might notice which courtier managed to squeeze in an extra couple of bows while walking backwards out of the audience chamber. Because bootlicking is now an important part of parliamentary procedure, MPs need tuition to help them. For example, Mr Harry Barnes, a Labour MP, discovered a letter from a Tory, Mr Simon Coombs, the Member for Swindon. This letter, it appeared, had been circulated to various MPs whose 'questions' were down for answer by the Secretary of State for Trade and Industry. It suggested that these MPs might care to attend a discussion with Ministers in the department shortly before Question Time began. 'Your contribution is much appreciated. It is an opportunity to make sure that the resulting exchanges will be beneficial to all,' he said, meaning beneficial to Ministers and toadies alike, though not of course in any way beneficial to the greater electorate.

Mr Barnes made quite a song and dance about this letter, so it's worth looking at the Trade and Industry question session which followed its discovery. Were the smarmy crawlers shamed into silence? Did they make even the faintest attempt to conceal their servility? Of course not. Mr Patrick Thompson asked about small businesses. He received a confusing list of numbers by way of reply, but this hardly mattered, since the question was really an excuse for him to 'pay tribute to the success of the government's policies'.

A Labour MP asked about people who had been billed thousands of pounds by British Telecom for overseas premium-rate phone calls, on sex lines for the most part, which they had not made. Mr Roy Thomason could hardly contain his excitement. A perfect poodling opportunity: 'Notwithstanding that difficulty, can my honourable friend confirm that BT's price levels have fallen by more than forty per cent in real terms since privatisation, which was opposed by the Opposition?' Well done, Roy. Not much chance of a job for you, I fear, but I do spy those magic initials 'OBE' after your name! It may stand for 'obsequious, bootlicking eunuch'. Either way, you've had your reward, so you can relax now. And so it went on.

Mrs Jacqui Lait spent the entire hour frothing with excitement about her question, number fifteen. Just in time, minutes before the end of the session, it was finally reached. It turned out to be a classic of its kind, worth studying in some detail because it was an almost perfect example of the genre.

It began with a phoney reference to her own seat, as if to imply that she had thought up the rigmarole herself. This was followed by a spurious question, meant to conform with the rules of order, which was succeeded by a verbose and convoluted centrepiece. It ended with the approved slogan of the week, dreamed up in Mayfair by advertising men in Armani suits and silly glasses, passed on to Central Office, and sent down the line to be obeyed by all troops:

'Does my right honourable friend accept that, in the constituency of Hastings and Rye, the tourism and rest-home sectors are two of the principal industries? Does he agree that if a national minimum wage were introduced in those two sectors, holiday-makers would go abroad rather than spend money in the United Kingdom, because tourism would be uncompetitive, and rest homes would have to put up prices, which would go straight on to public spending, and hence to higher taxation? Is not that another example of New Labour being new danger?'

What is so perfect about that fine example of the higher sycophancy is that precisely six days after Mrs Lait spoke, she was promoted to become the first-ever female Conservative Whip, and was the subject of admiring profiles in many newspapers. If she had shown the slightest independence of mind ('Does my right honourable friend agree that many people who work in tourist trade and in old people's homes lead desperately insecure lives, being paid pittances for jobs from which they could be sacked at any moment?'), she would have remained unnoticed and unremarked and unpromoted.

She is not alone. Innumerable greasers have also received shiny, spanking new jobs, no doubt as a direct result of their plucking and scraping. Mr James Clappison, Mr Simon Burns, Mr Gyles Brandreth, Ms Cheryl Gillan, Mrs Angela Browning – plus many, many more, including my old friend Michael Fabricant (q.v.) have all been translated to glory.

It does not invariably work. Greasing in some respects resembles a handicapped limbo-dancing contest ('How low can you go?') Some people are obliged to lower themselves more than others in order to atone for past crimes. A good example is Jacques Arnold (also q.v.) who supported John Redwood in the Tory leadership campaign of 1995, and is obliged therefore to crawl more than almost anyone else. Mr Arnold resembles Winston Smith, who dared to rebel, and then, in the terrible climax of 1984, came to realise that he loved Big Brother. At least Winston Smith had an excuse, in the Thought Police. Mr Arnold faced only the Conservative Whips.

There is a real strategy to oiling. If you want to turn yourself into liquid engineering, it's no use simply reading out what is on the piece of paper and hoping it will serve. You have to get a tone of enraged contempt into your voice, disguising your unctuousness as hard, tough-minded determination. 'Will. My. Right. Honourable. Friend. Agree with me! That! If this country were ever to have a Labour. Government. Inflicted on it! We could say goodbye to the prosperity of the last few years!'

You then sit down, chest heaving from your effort, mouth set grimly forward, scanning the benches in front as if your rage at their putative perfidy is almost enough to send you screaming across to their benches to throttle a few of them with piano wire, while in fact, they are chortling merrily at the ludicrous nature of your grovelling.

Mr Tony Blair has let it be known that he wants an end to all this. He proposes that Question Time should be genuinely informative, a means of keeping the public in touch with government, rather than a kind of communal whistling in the dark. Fat chance. If he becomes Prime Minister, the Tory Whips will distribute sheets explaining how, from day one of a new Labour government, every single problem faced by the country can be attributed to the hours, or days, or weeks of Labour misrule.

Labour MPs will feel obliged to reply in kind. New, left-of-centre poodles will appear. 'Does my right honourable friend not agree this shows the wonderful success of Labour's policies, following eighteen years of shameful neglect by the Party opposite?'

Possibly Mr Blair's Whips will take a different attitude from their Conservative predecessors. 'Don't like Blenkinsop, too bloody creepy if you ask me. Let's give the job to old Parkhouse – now he had the guts to ask a really tough question about interest rates the other day, left the Chancellor looking pretty silly... He's the kind of independent mind we need.'

But I doubt it.

NHS:
Plucked, Trust and Stuffed

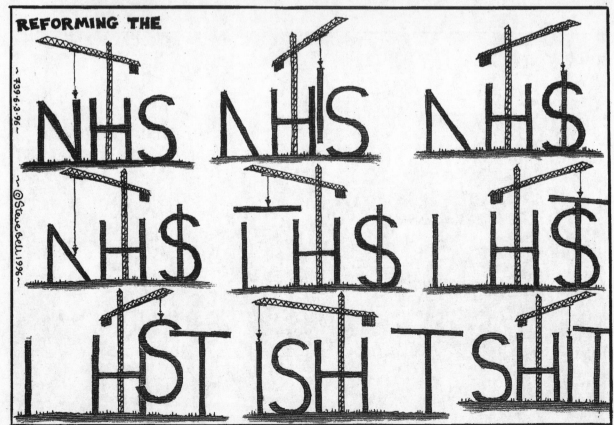

I AM THE LAW!

Because the two sides are so close together (Mr Howard is dreading the day when Mr Straw suggests the return of the stocks and ducking stools) the Home Secretary likes to imply that in fact Labour are the criminals' friend.

The unique awfulness of so much modern British politics finds its finest expression in debates on home affairs. Mr Howard the Home Secretary makes policy according to what he feels would go down well at a Conservative Party conference. Mr Straw, his opposite number of the Labour benches, appears to use the same yardstick. Indeed, some of his suggestions – a ban on the people who try to wash your windshield at busy road junctions, a curfew for teenagers – are so extreme one suspects that even a Tory conference would reject them. When Mrs Elizabeth Peacock suggested televised floggings for young offenders, to be shown at the same time as the National Lottery draw, one had the dismal feeling that this idea was so demented, so dreadfully unjust, that it would be official Labour policy in no time at all, with the sack for any Shadow Minister foolish enough to dispute it.

Now Home Affairs Question Time has become like some ancient horror movie; not a *Hammer* film of the sixties, in improbable

NO MADAM — I'M JUST PLEASED TO SEE YOU

colours, with busty starlets being bitten in the neck, but one of the sombre, black-and-white expressionist classics of the past.

Jack Straw is Jonathan Harker, the innocent young man sent with letters of introduction to the Count of Castle Dracula. Dusk is gathering as he walks upward, and clouds swirl down the mountain towards the tiny village, misting over his glasses.

Cackling squeegee merchants push towards him, waving their greasy, dripping sponges in his face. Knots of ragged children – many as young as ten – cluster at

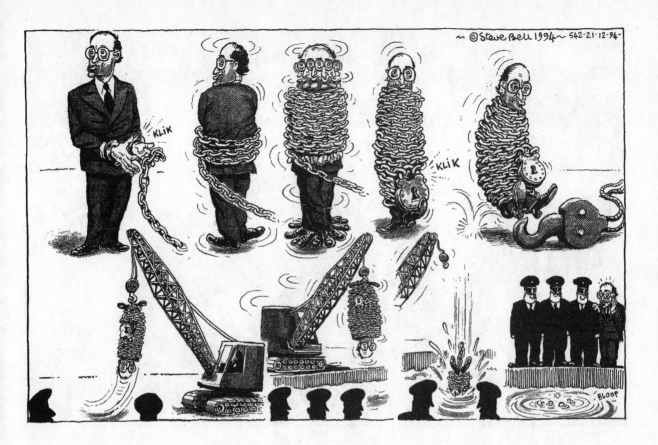

street corners, pointing at the stranger, jeering at his nervous, blinking eyes. He makes a mental note to suggest to his friend the Count that they should be summarily locked in the castle dungeons.

Outside the tavern stands a loutish fellow (David Evans, the Tory MP for Welwyn). He is bellowing at a crowd, trying to persuade the peasants to rise against the newcomers. 'We are sick an' tire' of immigrants who come 'ere, pay nuffink and take everyfink. Immigrants should stay 'ere for five years before they can use our 'Elf service. We know that lo' over there…[he points at Straw] …would let everybo'y in and it's the taxpier would pie the bill!'

Straw shudders and resumes his march up to the castle. But even as he climbs he can hear the voice of the sinister Tim Kirkhope (Con, Leeds NE), a Minister who is using the bigotry and ignorance of these simple peasants to pursue his own dark ends. 'I congratulate my friend on his robust remarks,' he says, silkily. 'If only the honourable gentleman and his colleagues opposite had been more supportive, we might have been able to deal with matters more effectively.'

It is cold now, icy cold, and the snow is falling hard – though it is not the only reason why Straw shivers as he continues on his quest.

Finally he reaches the castle and hammers on the door with his frozen fist. It is opened by a woman, a woman as wide as she is tall, capped by a mane of jet-black hair, quite unlike any creature he has ever seen. Yet he gives a start of recognition, for she is famed abroad as

the Count's most faithful servant, once christened 'Ann Widdecombe', but known to mortals by many other names – Doris Karloff, Belle Lugosi, Yvonne Chaney Jr, Glad the Impaler.

Glad is obsessed by the distant past. She shrieks at an innocent retainer (Greville Janner, Lab, Leicester W). 'He seems to think that we are responsible for overcrowding in prisons! Under the last Labour government there was a fifteen-per-cent increase in the prison population, but a capital funding cut!'

She shuffles down the dank, stone-flagged corridor to the dungeons, muttering as she goes: 'Callous neglect by the Opposition…neglect of overcrowding…' Her words disappear into the slime and mould which coat the thick black walls.

Inside the dungeons, manacled to a buttress, is David Ashby MP, condemned by a court for unnatural practices, his political life about to be brought to an end. Pathetically he tries to curry favour with Glad in the hopes of a reprieve. 'Does she not agree that this shows Conservative policies are the correct policies?' he whinges.

Glad screams back in a rage. 'We inherited from the last Labour government…,' she yells before the other prisoners drown her with their moaning and their jeers. For she has spent most of the past seventeen years living in a coffin, and to her, the events of seventeen years ago are as fresh in her mind as yesterday.

Darkness has now fallen outside. Nervously young Jack is sitting in an armchair in the castle's huge drawing room. In the hearth, a roaring fire. On the table, a jug full of what appears to be a particularly dark red wine. Suddenly he sees a tall, cloaked figure

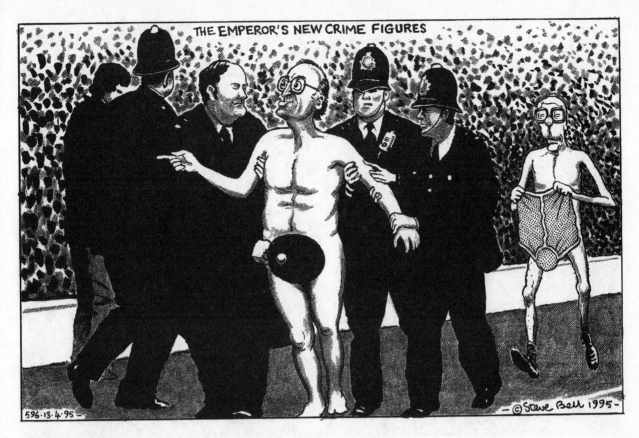

THE EMPEROR'S NEW CRIME FIGURES

596·13·4·95 —

— © Steve Bell 1995 —

standing in front of him, though he heard no footfall and noticed no shadow. It is the Count.

'Your schimm is full of difficilties,' he says in his weird, sibilant voice. 'The only kiffew the Libber Party is likely to impose is upon – you!'

Terror sweeps through the young traveller. Even as the Count smiles at him, he hears the mighty crash as the castle gate slams shut …

Just a reverie. Yet there is something not-of-this-planet-or-any-neighbouring-one-either about Mr Howard. Partly it is his accent, which turns almost every vowel into the letter 'i'. It is also ever so slightly sibilant, as if the air is being pushed past hollow-tipped fangs. 'Pipple hiv a right to ixpict proper p'licing!' he will say. In recent months the intrusive 'i' has begun to disappear, perhaps as the result of voice coaching, but at times of stress it is liable to return.

When Mr Howard is in trouble (this is rarely the result of his being assailed by Jack Straw) I am reminded of the woman who appeared in a recent controversial (a word which now means purely that the editor of the *Daily Mail* didn't like it) Channel 4 documentary about people with unusual perversions. One young woman, a necrophiliac, worked at an undertakers, so that she could take the clients home and enjoy them over the weekend. She would remove them to her mobile home and hang a notice outside saying, 'Don't come a-knockin' if this bus is a-rockin',' proving once again that a hard man really is good to find. In much the same way, Labour back-benchers like to jiggle up and down on Mr Howard, and there is

135

The tip of another Iceberg

FIRM BUT FAIR
ASYLUM &
IMMIGRATION
BILL

equally little sign that the recipient of these attentions enjoys them either.

On one happy occasion it was possible to study Mr Howard's performance through the eyes of Lord Whitelaw, a distant predecessor as Home Secretary. We soggy liberals always had a soft spot for Willie. Unlike Mr Howard, who makes wild and preposterous claims to the Tory Party conference, the then Mr Whitelaw appeared to offer them live chickens to bite, so to speak, while in fact promising nothing at all. He would talk at length about the appalling crime of murder and say how he fully understood and appreciated their overwhelming desire for a return to the death penalty. 'And that is why, when Parliament returns, we shall have a debate on the return of capital punishment – decided by a free vote of the House of Commons!' The delegates would cheer this mightily, even though it translates as: 'There is not the faintest chance of the rope being brought back in my lifetime!'

Mr Howard was making a statement about the embarrassing escapes from Parkhurst Prison. Lord Whitelaw sat in the peers' gallery, overlooking the Commons. His face does not mask his feelings; on the contrary, it demands no more interpretation or deconstruction than a Wonderbra hoarding.

Mr Howard would snap into his favourite mode, which is to announce that some dreadful problem has occurred on his watch, then announce that he will stop it! Immediately! Forthwith! 'Madam Spikker! Tickling the drug problem in our prissins is a difficult task!

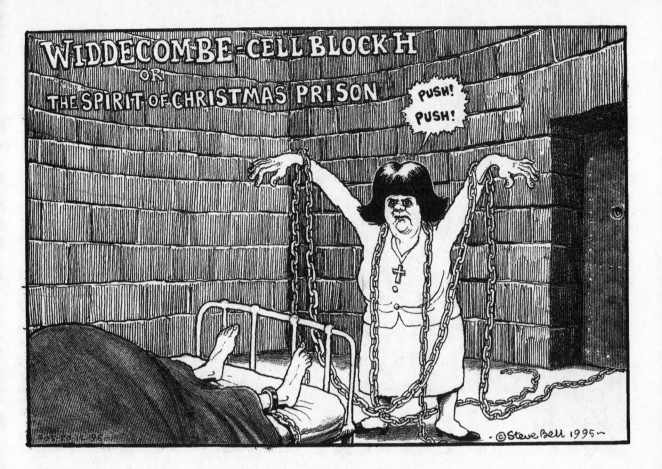

We cannot allow prissiners to diflict us from that task!' Lord Whitelaw discovered an intense interest in his own fingernails.

Mr Howard was outraged to be obliged to tell us that the prissiners had contrived to open no fewer than five doors and gates with a single forged key. Lord Whitelaw pursed his lips in displeasure, like a man who has sipped a fine malt whisky and discovered it to be cold tea.

The Home Secretary said that the fact that security measures had been largely ignored at Parkhurst was 'a cause for dismay'. Willie gazed into the middle distance, bearing an expression which might be called beatific cynicism.

Finally Mr Howard was able to tell us that – thank heavens – a scapegoat had been found. This was the governor of the prison, who had been kicked downstairs. Lord Whitelaw looked startled, and turned to a noble neighbour who, it seemed, had just that moment departed. Had he remained he might have learned some interesting new words. Instead, Lord Whitelaw scratched his bottom (his own, that is).

Having nominated the official scapegoat, Mr Howard saw no need to resign. He takes the view that he is responsible for policy and not for operations. Government policy is that everything should be for the best in the best of all possible worlds. If this proves not to be the case, it is clearly the result of operational failure, and not his fault.

BRITISH POLITICS EXPLAINED:
THE UNWRITTEN CONSTITUTION

©Steve Bell 1996 ~ 755·3·4·96

The ill-feeling between Mr Straw and Mr Howard is no doubt largely due to the fact that they agree about almost everything. In politics this does not promote cameraderie, but is known as stealing the other side's clothes. So Mr Howard's scorn for Mr Straw's promotion of curfews for young people is mainly caused by the fact that he didn't think of it first.

Usually, though not invariably, Mr Straw comes off the worse in debates with Mr Howard. Like many people who are deficient in their sense of humour, Mr Straw is also lacking in a sense of proportion. In politics, it is usually good advice to aim low. Don't declare in advance that your opponent is the most corrupt and venal politician since Caligula. Instead say that he is really rather silly. You have a better chance of proving it. Don't demand his resignation; instead insist that he remains in office, as the best guarantor of your own party's future electoral success.

This is how Mr Straw failed in the great confrontation with Mr Howard over the sacking of the head of the prison service. He was a caterer called Derek Lewis, who had in previous months been described by Labour MPs as 'unfit to run a whelk stall', but who had since his dismissal become, in their view, a national hero. Mr Straw had announced in advance of the debate that he possessed evidence so damning that Mr Howard would be obliged to resign. Of course he had nothing of the sort; he had a leaked civil service memo so ambiguous that Mr Howard himself was able to quote from it in his

own support.

As Tory MPs bayed, Mr Straw looked increasingly miserable, his great goggles in desperate need of a helpful squeegee merchant. The only time he appeared remotely happy was when Mr Howard interrupted him and so gave him something to bite upon – a rare example of a drowning Straw clutching at a man.

Because the two sides are so close together (Mr Howard is dreading the day when Mr Straw suggests the return of the stocks and ducking stools to secondary schools), the Home Secretary likes to imply that in fact Labour are the criminals' friend, soft-hearted do-gooders who would excuse a multiple rapist on the grounds that he had suffered a difficult childhood.

The normal Tory approach is to point out that Labour voted against many of their 'crime prevention' measures. The implication is that do-badders, caught by the police, would say, 'You got me bang to rights, all right, but I was led into a life of crime by the failure of the Opposition front bench to support Clause 8, paragraph 14, in the Criminal Law Bill (1993).'

Ludicrous, of course, yet Mr Howard's blustering also terrifies Labour politicians. They fear him appearing on TV to say, 'It is the Libber Party which voted against public disimbowelling for litter bugs! You kinnot trust Libber on krimm!' When a Labour back-bencher pointed out that, with all those video cameras in our streets, we were now more spied upon than any other people in Europe,

— AFTER GUSTAVE DORE — © Steve Bell 1988

including the citizens of the old Soviet empire, Mr Howard said, 'Thire spikks the true voice of the Libber Party! Antidiluvian views while Kinnsivattives are trying to reduce krimm! You kinnot trust Libber on krimm!'

The most marginal musing on the subject of krimm is interpreted as a desire to provide muggers with free holidays in Florida. When Mr Tony Blair suggested that there were worse crimes than shop-lifting a loaf of bread to feed a hungry family, Mr Howard became apoplectic in that peculiarly unreal way he has. 'The Lidder of the Oppisition his bin going up and down the kintry making speeches which excuse shoplifting. He will go down in hist'ry as "The Pilferers' Friend".'

One wonders how hist'ry will record it. 'Mr Tony Blair (b. 1953) was usually known as "The Pilferer's Friend". The violent krimm wave which engulfed Britain in the 1990s was blamed largely on his view that there wasn't too much wrong with nicking the odd Rolo for your kid…'

THE FLASH IN THE PAN

Mr Justice Scott said, in effect, that the government had been caught bang to rights. Guilty, guilty, guilty. Guilty on all counts.

The Scott Report investigated claims that the government had connived in selling arms to the Iraqi regime of Saddam Hussein, plus allegations that Ministers would have let a group of businessmen go to jail rather than admit what had been going on. They had, it was alleged, also deliberately misled Parliament by pretending that the guidelines for sales to Iraq had been changed.

Mr Justice Scott said, in effect, that the government had been caught bang to rights. Guilty, guilty, guilty. Guilty on all counts.

This could have been a public-relations disaster, which is the only type of disaster the present government recognises. (In their eyes, events, policies, statements and decisions have no independent moral standing, indeed no real existence at all outside the public's perception; thus they can be judged only by the extent to which they affect poll results.)

There was only one solution, and it turned out to be the one

always favoured by this government: blame the Opposition. This might seem ridiculous, if you were to take into account the fact that the Opposition has no authority in these matters, but that is the merest quibble to the Conservative front bench.

The task of blaming the Opposition was made easier by the way that the Scott Report is written in two languages: English and British. English is the successful, demotic tongue spoken all over the world. British is a quite different language which uses much of the same vocabulary but communicates the thought processes of the mandarin classes, the higher civil service, and some of the more old-fashioned politicians. It bears some relation to the different language constructions which may be used in Japan only by persons of high status.

A good example of British came just before the Scott Report was published, when Sir Robin Butler spoke to a Commons select committee on changes in the civil service. Many of the questions he was asked by MPs were in English, but almost all his replies were in British. For instance, a Labour MP asked whether he agreed with Sir Geoffrey Howe that the Scott Inquiry had been 'procedurally flawed'.

Sir Robin replied, 'I have made no public criticism of the procedures of the Inquiry, throughout.' This is British for 'I have been spitting nails in private.'

Another MP tried to find out how much power and authority Mr Michael Heseltine had accumulated as Deputy Prime Minister. Sir Robin replied courteously that Mr Heseltine had been 'taking, as

part of his activities, the day-to-day civil service'. This did not, of course, include such matters as senior appointments: 'There I still deal directly with the Prime Minister.' An English–British interpreter would have translated this as: 'If you think that Hezza is in charge of anything that matters, you need your head read.'

The point about British is that it is never rude about anyone. Words such as 'incompetent', 'overambitious' and 'dishonest' are banned. Instead it is necessary to find circumlocutions which – and this is the difficult part even for practised speakers – sound as if they are actually unstinted praise. For instance, at another point, Sir Robin was asked if it was true that the new Deputy Prime Minister felt civil servants should be more numerate. He replied, 'I do know that Mr Heseltine does act through the presentation of diagrams and figures, and would like more of that rather than great long essays, or verbiage.'

The joy of that sentence, which appears to imply that Mr Heseltine is a robust sort of fellow who wants to get straight to the facts, is that in its original British, it has the opposite meaning, to wit: 'Fellow is barely able to read. But we can get anything past him if we turn it into a couple of statistics, a graph and a pie chart.'

In the same way, Sir Richard Scott used English – the tongue of the artisan, yeoman and rude peasant – to lambast the government, but British to defend it. Mr William Waldegrave, who in English had sent out dozens of fibbing letters to MPs, was, in British, not guilty of any intention to mislead.

The government used these findings – that Ministers were simultaneously responsible for the scandal and yet entirely blameless – by granting itself eight days to read the report in advance (quite a lot of work; it weighs seventeen pounds) while giving it to Robin Cook, the Opposition spokesman, just three hours before publication. Like W. C. Fields reading the Bible on his deathbed – 'I'm looking for loopholes' – Ministers were searching for the passages in British which exonerated them. Back-benchers knew nothing. At 3.30 they scurried from the Chamber to queue for their copies. (First in line was Edwina Currie. She immediately signed her copy, 'Best wishes, Edwina,' and handed it back. Sorry, I made that up.)

It led to one of those increasingly rare occasions when the House of Commons really is the nation's debating forum. Heaven knows, this scarcely ever happens these days. If it is the result of MPs not knowing anything whatever about the subject in hand, perhaps we should keep them in ignorance more often.

So almost all MPs were startled when Mr Ian Lang rose to give the government's account. The report was quite unexpected, consisting of 1,800 pages of praise for Ministers' honesty, integrity and sincerity, interrupted only by occasional murmurs of distress about the way events had actually turned out.

'He makes no criticism of government policy,' Mr Lang purred. There had been no attempt to gag anyone, no conspiracy to jail innocent men. The central charges were unfounded.

144

How, we mused, could any of us have got hold of the idea that they might be all too founded? Of course, it was the fault of the Opposition.

'For three years [Ministers] have had to endure abuse and attacks on their honour and integrity of the most offensive and unpleasant nature…they now stand wholly vindicated.'

There was an uneasy stirring on the Labour benches. They must have felt like Timon of Athens's guests, invited to a banquet and served bowls of tepid water.

Mr Lang vaguely admitted that Scott felt a few matters might, in retrospect, have been better handled. (He reminded me of those old-fashioned motoring correspondents who saw their job as boosting British products at every opportunity. 'If this car has a fault, and heaven knows there are few enough, it could be that the ashtray might be a trifle more commodious.') The government would be looking into these matters. Meanwhile, the important business was to rub Labour's nose in its own moral turpitude.

Labour MPs were suffused in gloom. Then Robin Cook rose. It was probably the best parliamentary performance by anyone since the 1982 election. It must have been deeply galling to Mr Cook's many opponents, such as the Conservative Party and various bookmakers, and more so to his enemies (P. Mandelson).

Mr Cook had read the report alone and without assistance. He was shut away in a room without refreshment. However, he had used to the time to discover those parts which had been written in English.

145

'I have spent the last three hours studying it, and I do not recognise the report I read in the statement we have just heard.' He recited Scott's charges: Mr Waldegrave's deliberate failure to let MPs know what was going on, the secret shift in policy, the way that the government had known perfectly well that pipes were being exported from Britain to create a supergun, and the fashion in which Ministers were told they had to keep secret policies secret even if it meant that the accused men could not defend themselves.

Labour morale soared. They began to cheer Mr Cook, and even to whistle at each choice new paragraph he had discovered. They even waved their copies of the report in the air, a hazardous act which could have induced hernias in some older Members.

Mr Cook has been called (by me) a vandalised garden gnome. But on this occasion he was more like a featherweight boxer, bobbing and weaving, appearing underneath his clumsier opponent purely in order to land another punch.

His *coup de grâce* came when he pointed out that Ministers had blamed civil servants for failing to draft the correct replies. Yet those same civil servants had been told that if they replied to that, they must not in turn criticise Ministers.

Mr Cook's voice rose to a squeak of moral outrage. 'How dare they criticise civil servants while ordering these civil servants not to criticise Ministers?' He sat down to a storm of applause from his own side, and a morose silence from the other.

Mr Lang's reply was feeble. It tottered forward as if supported by a Zimmer frame. Mr Cook had spent ten minutes talking to the Press before reading the report: true, but hardly the point. Absurdly, Mr Lang added, 'You have now blighted your career in this House!' On the contrary, some Labour MPs were now wondering whether Mr Cook might one day make a good leader, in spite of his appearance.

In the days that followed various Opposition Members tried to return to the attack. Mr Blair found the government 'knee-deep in dishonour'. Soon they would be waist-deep in dishonour, then up to their necks in dishonour, and finally found dead in bed, choking on their own dishonour, like rock group drummers. In the end, on the end, the government had a majority of one. Jeffrey Archer quoted Churchill: 'One is enough.' He was wrong. Sometimes one is far, far too few.

WILLIAM WALDEGRAVE "HE WAS A WASTE OF SPACE"

SEX, LIES AND TORY PR

Tories may have most advertisers on their side, but they seem to have lost their way with public relations. These days everything they touch goes wrong.

We used to think of the Conservatives as the Party which understood advertising. Most advertisers, at least the richer kind who head the big agencies, are Tories themselves, and are delighted to offer their services.

(Of course there are left-wingers in advertising too. Many copywriters, the 'creative' people who come to work in jeans and trainers, have vaguely left-of-centre sympathies. One such was Salman Rushdie whom I watched, long before *Midnight's Children* made him famous, address an anti-racism awareness rally at the Friends' Meeting Hall near Euston Station. He was introducing a short advertising film which, he said, demonstrated the innate racism of the British advertising industry. It was a spoof of the film *Zulu*, in which the black hordes offer the defending Welshmen just two weeks to get used to the new, milder taste of Silk Cut cigarettes before killing the lot. What particularly offended Mr Rushdie was the fact that the Zulus were played by white actors in make-up.

He went on to say that British advertising was so racist that no

147

black people were ever depicted in commercials as ordinary folk. There were murmurs of shocked agreement at this aperçu, except from a small group of East Enders, possibly sent to infiltrate the meeting by the National Front. One of them shouted out, 'Worrabout Smarties, then?' 'I think,' said Salman Rushdie, 'that proves my point. You can remember the single occasion that a black person was shown as an ordinary consumer.'

'Worrabout the Gas Board?' shouted another racist. 'Yeah, and how abaht Birdseye fish fingers, eh?' yelled another. Mr Rushdie tried to calm them down. 'The fact that you can remember these very isolated examples proves how rare it is...'

'Vauxhall! Worthingtons! *Daily Mirror*! Electrolux!' shouted the East Enders. 'Yes,' Mr Rushdie countered feebly, 'there are so few you can remember them all.' 'Gillette! Dixons! Gibbs SR! Wall's ice cream!' they chanted, and the more Mr Rushdie flannelled in reply, the more they jeered. 'Admit it, son, you don't know what you're bleeding talking about,' one of the horrid racists said.

I have described this incident at length – I am sure I have misremembered most of the brand names, but otherwise the story is entirely accurate – because it taught me so much about the way people with strong views, political or otherwise, perceive the world around them. Convinced that British advertising was endemically racist, as he believes our whole nation to be, Salman Rushdie did not notice that coloured people appeared increasingly often in TV commercials. The horrid racists, equally certain that the blacks were taking over, noticed every vaguely dark face appearing for two seconds in the corner of the screen. The effect is much the same in the House of Commons. Facts which do not fit the theory disappear unnoticed, consigned to the speaker's mental oubliette; those which seem to confirm it assume overwhelming significance. As with the question of whether British advertising is racist, the truth is generally somewhere in the middle, but in politics that is the one position which no one is allowed to occupy.)

Tories may have most advertisers on their side, but they seem to have lost their way with public relations. These days everything they touch goes wrong. Take their new tabloid 'good news' newspaper. It was called *Look!* and had a bright, manic feel, a cross between *Hello!* and a fanzine, such as *Rubberwear Monthly*.

One of the great saloon-bar myths is that someone once produced a newspaper which contained only good news, but nobody bought it. In fact, it was a religious publication, and the good news tended to be along the lines of 'Stop Press: Jesus died for your sins.' As Peregrine Worsthorne once pointed out, the good news is in the papers, but it is to be found among the advertisements. Alongside items about Bosnia and interest-rate rises there is the excellent news that flights to New York are now cheaper than ever, or that the new Volvo has an advanced anti-lock braking system.

However, nobody ever needed to buy *Look!* because it was given away by Conservative Central Office. The good news it contained was relentless. 'Tax bonanza for millions. Spring is in the air as cash windfalls and Budget cocktail deliver a boost'; 'Good News Britain, as seen by an admiring world' (apparently foreigners are united in

148

awe of our achievements); 'Britain poised to lead the way in a new wave of super technology' and 'We're now a nation of happy shoppers!'

We were invited to thank the government for the success of the dancer Darcey Bussell, who appeared beaming on the front page ('Schools Minister Cheryl Gillan has unveiled a plan to allow two hundred more children…to attend famous schools like the Royal Ballet') and on page five there was a picture of Cheryl, looking winsome. Once she was known only as one of Westminster's crack greasers; now she is the cause of a national artistic renaissance.

Naturally there was no mention of crime (except for its abolition): 'Howard's get-tough stance calls time on repeat offenders'), or of poverty, or the arms-for-Iraq débâcle, or the beef crisis, or home repossessions, or Black Wednesday, or even the great kash-for-kwestions scandal which at least proved that in Conservative Britain there are opportunities for everyone to get rich, even including MPs.

In short, *Look!* depicted a Britain as real as the Big Rock Candy Mountain. The launch proved to be a disaster, since Ms Bussell, among others, had not given permission for her name to be used, and she made it clear that she resented it very much.

Then there was the even more embarrassing 'Labour Hypocrisy'. This was a board game, similar in appearance to Monopoly, but any sporting excitement it might have engendered was dissipated by the political propaganda which suffused every minute of the game. The

playing pieces were outdated Labour archetypes: a stupid trade
unionist, a fat feminist, a bearded weirdie, and so on. You went
round the board collecting points for political correctness (PCPs) and
for hypocrisy. For example, you might land on a square marked
'hypocrite' and receive a card saying, 'You tell us that being tough on
crime and tough on the causes of crime is not an empty slogan. So
why did Labour consistently vote against, or refuse to support,
tough measures to combat crime?' You scored more points for
landing on Islington ('Blair's Blunder Borough, which has twice the
debts of Albania after forty years of Communism…' You could pick
up three hypocrisy points by landing on Bromley and sending your
child to a selective school.

It was tedious beyond anything anyone could imagine. Even the
Conservatives seemed to realise this, and decided not to market the
game in shops. Instead they ordered just a hundred copies from their
own printworks, and sent them out as prizes for local Conservative
Associations. One can vaguely imagine the scene: the winners
inviting their friends round for a Hock and Hypocrisy party, the
jollity as the game is opened and the rules read, the rapidly dawning
awareness that it would be infinitely more amusing to spend the
evening betting on snail racing.

But the greatest public-relations disaster of them all was the spoof
manifesto, entitled 'The Road to Ruin'. It was launched at a press
conference at which Michael Heseltine and the Party Chairman,

Brian Mawhinney, desperately tried to perform as a double comedy act. The document itself was designed to be deft satire, inserting the stiletto of humour into the ribcage of New Labour.

But watching politicians try to be funny is like seeing a carthorse doing dressage. It's embarrassing. You wish you weren't there. And yet somehow, 'The Road to Ruin' was funny, though unconsciously. It was tremendously, thunderously camp. It brought to mind all the backstage bitching of the old sitcom, *It Ain't Half Hot, Mum*. Large parts of it could be read out in a fey, Kenneth Williams voice at Labour Party meetings. It's a matter of getting the emphases right:

'One of the first acts of a Labour government will be to end Britain's shameful opt-out from the social chapter. We believe that for Britain to enjoy falling unemployment while unemployment rises across Europe could lead to unacceptable tensions, and we know what those lead to, don't we, dears? You'd better watch what you're putting in the old man's tea!' (I have added slightly to the original text, but feel I have been true to its spirit.)

Or take their brief summary of Labour policies at the beginning of the booklet. You have to remember that this is meant to be a biting lampoon:

'A new stakeholder economy in which everyone (trade unions, pressure groups and so on) is included and no one is excluded.

'New communities so that everyone is in bed by 10.00 p.m., and not out shopping, as they are under the Tories.

'A new Europe in which Britain is really nice, and gets its way by agreeing to everyone else's suggestions.'

Later, on page twenty-one:

'Labour policies will ensure that despite devolution, England and Wales will continue to benefit from the experience of people like Gordon Brown, Gavin Strang and Donald Dewar. To make quite sure that these Scottish MPs don't lose touch with the rest of the UK, they will pay the lower rate of income tax…'

Oooh, get her! Put our knickers on the wrong way round this morning, did we? Or take the mincing line which whipped the Labour Party into a cappuccino of fake anger, the one which was alleged to be a tasteless attack on David Blunkett: 'We think the provision of free eye tests to millionaires is a health priority.' Whoops a daisy, dearie!

Sometimes we leave the backstage sniping at an all-male revue, and find ourselves in the playground of a girls' school, that theatre of vicious social combat. 'New Labour also believes that a new vibrant Britain must give the people of the East Midlands a chance to realise their burning desire for a regional parliament, which is exactly the kind of dumb thing you'd expect a stupid dork who wears braces on her teeth like Sophie Pettigrew to say…'

NEW LABOUR:
If the Policy Suits – Change it!

New Labour is a cult as well as a Party. Like any group of weirdos living in the mountains of Oregon, it has its grinning guru in Tony Blair, and a more sinister, shadowy enforcer in Peter Mandelson.

New Labour is a cult as well as a Party. Like any group of weirdos living in the mountains of Oregon, it has its grinning guru in Tony Blair, and a more sinister, shadowy enforcer in Peter Mandelson. Like all cults it demands total loyalty to the Supreme Leader; the certainty that he cannot be wrong gives members of the sect a sense of comfort and assurance, rather like the more old-fashioned Roman Catholics feel about the Pope. His frequent and sometimes alarming policy changes are his equivalent of bedding the young female members; acceptance of behaviour which might have seemed disgraceful in the years before you joined the cult is perceived as proof of your commitment.

Born-again Christians often define themselves by the past they rejected. New Labourites are proud of the fact that they once flew the Red Flag from their town hall; that they twinned their council with some desperate village in a Marxist-led hell-hole; that they once spent weeks in twig houses near Greenham Common, painting their faces and getting in touch with the Earth Mother. Now they have capacious shoulder-bags filled with think-tank reports about the need to tackle child poverty, together with position papers from Gordon Brown explaining how child poverty can only be tackled when resources allow.

But the cult rejects no one. All can be saved, even those who were never lost in the first place. Here's an archetypal New Labour remark, from the Brighton Party Conference. Judith Church, a new New Labour MP, described how she had been out canvassing in her constituency and had intended to skip a house which had a large new BMW in the front driveway. Fortunately she hadn't, because the owner turned out to be an enthusiastic Labour convert. 'Who are these people who haven't voted Labour, who have never voted Labour?' she asked. 'Tories!' shouted some old Labour dinosaur from the back.

Ms Church was undeterred. She began to dream on behalf of BMW owners, a maligned and misunderstood group. 'The BMW owner doesn't think he's rich. He doesn't feel he is going to be able to hold on to his house much longer, or to his job. He has suffered more under the Tories than under us.'

This heartwarming reverie (one half-expected Ms Church to begin a charity appeal: for the money you might waste on a few artesian wells in Africa, you could provide a BMW owner with a set of leopardskin seat covers…) was interrupted by Mr Roy Hattersley. Mr Hattersley is something of a hate-figure to New Labour. Once they felt he was one of them. Now he is an apostate, reviling the sect and implying that the Supreme Leader is little better than a power-crazed fraud.

153

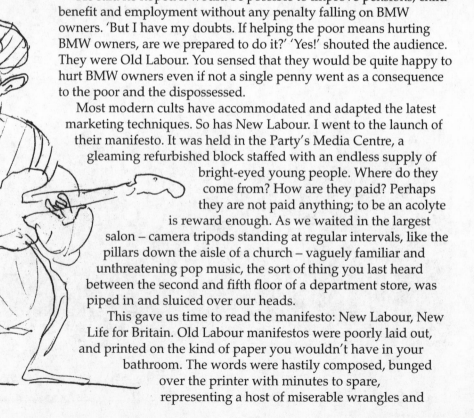

He said he hoped it would be possible to improve pensions, child benefit and employment without any penalty falling on BMW owners. 'But I have my doubts. If helping the poor means hurting BMW owners, are we prepared to do it?' 'Yes!' shouted the audience. They were Old Labour. You sensed that they would be quite happy to hurt BMW owners even if not a single penny went as a consequence to the poor and the dispossessed.

Most modern cults have accommodated and adapted the latest marketing techniques. So has New Labour. I went to the launch of their manifesto. It was held in the Party's Media Centre, a gleaming refurbished block staffed with an endless supply of bright-eyed young people. Where do they come from? How are they paid? Perhaps they are not paid anything; to be an acolyte is reward enough. As we waited in the largest salon – camera tripods standing at regular intervals, like the pillars down the aisle of a church – vaguely familiar and unthreatening pop music, the sort of thing you last heard between the second and fifth floor of a department store, was piped in and sluiced over our heads.

This gave us time to read the manifesto: New Labour, New Life for Britain. Old Labour manifestos were poorly laid out, and printed on the kind of paper you wouldn't have in your bathroom. The words were hastily composed, bunged over the printer with minutes to spare, representing a host of miserable wrangles and

unhappy compromises. Now the Party realises that a manifesto is as much a marketing tool as the brochure which advertises a new car. The image is far more important than the language.

Thus the latest manifesto is filled with colour pictures of delightful, optimistic people in delightful, optimistic settings. A father takes his baby on a carousel; a lovable old fellow in a cloth cap wheels his bicycle past a lush green meadow; a hawk-eyed fighter pilot waits in his cockpit; an expectant little girl listens in a classroom; and three blissful small children sit safely strapped in the back of their parents' car, their faces illuminated as if by a passing space ship, looking forward to a wonderful family outing.

The curious thing is that these pictures – and the busy operating theatre, and the bustling high-tech factories – could just as easily appear in the Conservative manifesto to illustrate what a contented country we live in.

Possibly the same pictures have appeared in Tory advertising. Certainly the mood of the Labour leaflet (at £10 for forty pages it works out at roughly twenty-five times per page more costly than a Jeffrey Archer novel in hardback) is precisely the same as a Conservative Party broadcast. There are no crumbling schools, no peeling hospital wards, no wasteland occupied by unemployed youths kicking stones or worse. All polls show that people vote for politicians who are optimistic about the future, rather than those who are gloomy about the past. That's how Ronald Reagan won all his elections so handsomely. The underlying message of all new propaganda is this: 'Look, we know things aren't so bad under the

Tories. But they need tinkering with, and anyway, it's our turn. All right?'

The production symbolised the enormous shift in the Party's belief in marketing. In the past, TV broadcasts were made by sympathetic technicians who would do the work for a pie and a pint. On one occasion, a Labour MP had been recruited to dub the voice-overs. This was to be in a small studio lodged somewhere in one of the sleazier streets of Soho. As the MP peered at the labels on the bell pushes ('Large chest on view', 'French teacher – strict methods') a passing policeman asked sarcastically, 'Can I help you, sir?' The MP raised himself to his full height and declared, 'I am making a party political broadcast on behalf of the Labour Party.' 'Blimey,' said the policeman, 'I've never heard it called that before.'

Back at the manifesto launch, the Shadow Cabinet marched in with unnerving speed. (There must have been a choreographer somewhere in the background: 'Come on, darlings, briskly, briskly, it's a launch, not a funeral…') They spread out on the platform, first those who you probably haven't heard of, and Tony Blair hopes you never will hear of. Then the famous names, the Harmans, the Browns, the Cooks and the Mowlams.

(One problem for New Labour is that Old Labour persists in voting for all the people Mr Blair would prefer to disappear. At Shadow Cabinet elections they figure out exactly which candidates he would like to have at his side, then vote against them. Those he regards as a terrible waste of space receive generous block votes from the disgruntled comrades. For instance, after the 1995 elections,

celebrating Labour MPs were lined up in the Strangers' Bar to congratulate Joan Lestor, who had just increased her vote by twenty-five per cent as a direct consequence of Mr Blair's satraps demanding her removal.)

Then the unseen choreographer told them to disperse ('All righty, darlings, take ten, but don't go away, we may need you later') and they sat by the side of the hall acting as a claque, laughing exaggeratedly at the Leader's jokes, and jeering the questions they didn't like – a curious and amusing role reversal for us hacks. The three remaining on the platform, Messrs Blair, Brown and Cook, began to introduce each other. I had time to notice Mr Blair's eyes. When he knows he is being watched, by someone he's talking to or through a camera, these are both bright and shining, matching the gleam of his orthodontically perfect teeth. When he is off-camera, they are strange and remarkable. The right eye becomes dark, hooded and sunken. The left, by contrast, bulges with a manic gleam – the same gleam that Mrs Thatcher also had in one eye. Is he her love child? They are the right age, and it could account for a lot.

Mr Blair addressed us. He was concerned to point out that New Labour had no relation to Old Labour, but was linked, by right of apostolic succession, to Ancient Labour. 'Keir Hardie would sign up to [the manifesto],' he said. (This person is no relation to 'Kir' Ardit, the

popular Dordogne bartender.) 'Attlee would sign up to it. Harold Wilson would sign up to it,' he added, not pointing out that all these heroes are conveniently dead.

Would Keir Hardie have signed up to the ringing proposition on taxation in the manifesto? 'Consistent with the high-quality services we need, you should be able to keep as much of the money you have earned to spend as you like.' Probably so. The people Hardie spoke for never paid income tax. Indeed, no working people at all did until the Second World War. In those days income tax was a mark of prestige; people boasted about it, rather as in the late 1980s they boasted about the size of their rates bill.

Mr Blair has realised an important truth. In the global economy, there are few specific promises that can be made about anything. Governments do not, on the whole, run their countries but they act as facilitators for the international corporations who take the important decisions. When Siemens, the German electronics giant, announced that it was building a £1.1 billion plant near Newcastle, the managing director specified that the company liked having – not his exact words but certainly his precise meaning – a docile, under-paid workforce. These days governments impose tax levels in the same way as restaurants impose their charges: they can demand whatever they like, but not if they want the customers to return.

So Mr Blair and his Party have evolved a style of rhetoric which makes few if any specific promises. (The few they do make are important but essentially marginal, such as smaller class sizes and

faster imprisonment for juvenile offenders.) What they offer are
buzz-phrases, warm words, gestures rather than pledges. Party
officials insist that these are repeated over and over again. 'New
Labour – New Life for Britain'; 'Hope in place of fear'. They have
realised what the Americans spotted decades ago: the electorate is
not taking notes, and if you say something a hundred times, there
will still be a hermit living on the Mull of Kintyre who has not yet
heard it.

These phrases are as sinuous and slippery as a trout. When the
Tories promised not to raise taxes, then raised taxes, they could be
criticised as hypocrites or incompetents. But what voter could ever
say, 'Here, you promised new life for Britain. But what do you call
this?' No one can write to Labour HQ demanding their money back
on the grounds that hope had not replaced fear in their personal life.

Mr Blair has managed this in a dramatic form. As his speeches
progress, he abolishes verbs. At the Brighton conference he uttered a
total of 196 sentences without verbs. The speech becomes less of an
address than a chant: 'Decent people. Good people. Patriotic
people… New Britain. The Party renewed. The country renewed.
New Labour.'

He does the same in every important speech. At the manifesto
launch: 'Fairness at work. Practical proposals. In crime, tough on
crime, tough on the causes of crime. In Europe: leadership, not
isolation.' 'In every area, policy is New Labour.' (Sorry, that does
contain a verb, but in some mysterious way feels as if it doesn't.)

SHUT UP AND GET ON WITH YOUR **EXTRA HOMEWORK!**

Daddy, what did YOU die of in the Great War On Drugs?

'Smaller classes. Shorter waiting lists. A turning point in British politics. New Labour. New life for Britain.'

For too long, one feels, the Party's energy wasted. On verbs. On doing words. For the British people now, no more verbs. But feelgood words. Happy words. Tough on verbs, tough on the causes of verbs. New words, non-verbal words, new Britain.

Yet little that is concrete has been proposed. Like so much of the manifesto, each verbless phrase offers a fine aspiration, worthy in every way, utterly estimable and entirely vague.

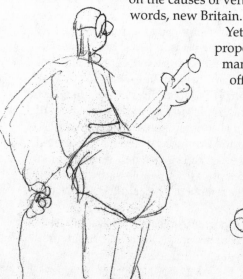

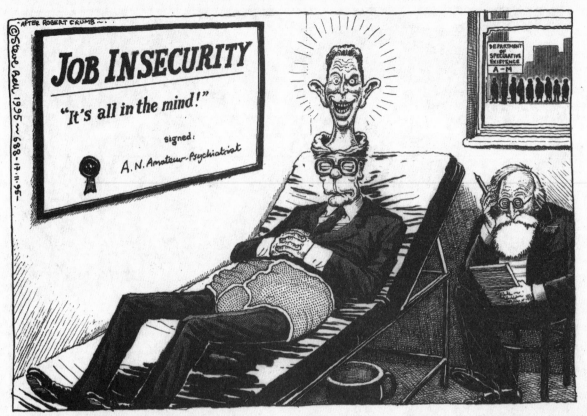

THE *'Rolls Royce'* OF PARLIAMENTS

On some days, we sketchwriters provide the only reporting of the Chamber. But we are not concerned with balanced reportage, merely with cheap and demeaning jokes. As soon as we have found them, we depart to our terminals by way of the cafeteria.

The House of Commons Chamber is a sad place for most of the time these days. You might catch the riotous screaming of Prime Minister's Question Time and imagine the place was alive and throbbing, but the noise you hear is like some young persons' party held in the grounds of a ruined abbey, each shout and yell mocking the solemnity of the ancient walls.

In the past, making a speech in the House was the most important thing an MP could do. He would spend days, if not weeks, preparing it. It would be listened to by a large and appreciative House. Afterwards, the MP could expect the congratulations of his colleagues, or, if he had done badly, a sombre and worrying silence. (Sometimes, it is said, a new Member who did not know the joke would be told that he had made a 'Rolls-Royce' of a speech. Only the more cruel would explain this meant that it went on forever and no one could hear it.)

There were certain names – Enoch Powell, Michael Foot and suprisingly, Brian Walden (it is quite unfair to suggest that these days Mr Walden, no longer an MP, is merely a shill for British Telecom; he used to represent the bookmakers, as well) – who could 'fill the Chamber'. Their names would appear on the monitor screens around the House, and Members would drop their work, put down their drinks, and scurry to hear them speak.

There is no back-bencher who can make that claim now. Indeed the only front-benchers who even attract interest from the passing trade are Robin Cook and Michael Heseltine. Geoffrey Howe, Norman Lamont and Margaret Thatcher made compelling resignation speeches, but none were famed for their oratorical skills while they were still in office. Gordon Brown can be funny, but doesn't often try. I admired Edwina Currie for her speech on lowering the gay age of consent, but mostly for her courage in standing up to the yobbos on her own side. Peter Mandelson is said to be the second-most (the most, according to some) powerful person in the Labour Party, famed for his secretive, behind-the-scenes briefings, yet his public utterances are sometimes scarcely literate.

But nowadays, making a speech is a fringe activity. It ranks in prestige somewhere above an appearance on *Sky News* and considerably below an interview on *Breakfast with Frost*. Oratory is not quite dead, but is perhaps like Walt Disney, waiting on ice until the cure has been invented.

Twenty years ago, when *The Times* was still *The Times*, and the political editor once began a thunderous front-page lead story with the word 'Notwithstanding…', the paper devoted an entire page to the day's business in the House and had a staff of more than a dozen people to fill it. All the broadsheet papers had similar, if smaller,

teams. Debates in the House were considered important political events in themselves and the Great Panjandrums of the Parliamentary Lobby (most of whom would be offered, and some would accept, knighthoods) could be seen sitting in their pomp, mightier almost than anyone on the benches below them, like the Headmaster of Eton watching fives practice. Now they rarely drag themselves away from *Channel 4 News* to hear a mere MP speak, and the Chamber has become a side-bar to the main political news.

It is as if football reporting consisted of endless wrangles about the new England manager, with only a throwaway paragraph to say that the team had lost 6–5 on penalties in the European semi-final. Sometimes I wander into the Press Gallery – even at a time when the Speaker has had to limit speeches to ten minutes in order to accommodate all the Members who want to speak – and find four other people there: the attendant, the Press Association reporter, the Hansard stenographer and the person waiting to take over from the Hansard stenographer. The Hansard they produce now costs £5 a copy, an absurd price which hovers between what it costs to print and what it ought to cost to buy. In fact, you would have to pay more than £800 a year for the Commons alone, and what librarian would think MPs' words were worth more than the hundred new books he could buy with the money?

On some days, we sketchwriters provide the only reporting of the Chamber. But we are not concerned with balanced reportage, merely with cheap and demeaning jokes. As soon as we have found them, we depart to our terminals by way of the cafeteria. As Baroness Young put it in the House of Lords, during a debate on declining standards in British public life, 'Some clever political correspondent gives you a ten-inch column, saying isn't that clever, the Minister knocked off the back-bencher, or the back-bencher knocked off the Minister.'

Proud as I occasionally am of my ten-inch column, I recognised myself in that complaint and to a large extent sympathised. Back in the seventies the sketch was the blob of cream, your reward for ploughing through the serious stuff. Now it is sometimes all the Chamber has to offer. The Strangers' Gallery is still full for Prime Minister's Question Time, as seen on TV. The participants appear to the same excited applause as the minor soap star walking on as Buttons in the Croydon pantomime, but it empties soon afterwards, even for what would in the past have been thought high-class entertainment: Cook *v.* Rifkind, Heseltine *v.* Prescott. By the end of the day there may be no one there but a a handful of puzzled tourists, drunks and schoolchildren whose teachers could not get them into anything more exciting.

MPs themselves still turn out for the big events – for three-line whips they are obliged to. (Heaven knows what will happen when the House catches up with the twentieth century – some time in the twenty-second, no doubt – and allows MPs to send their votes electronically from wherever they are.) Most will deign to listen to the two speeches before the vote, if only to assure themselves that they really have been paying attention to the arguments. On high-profile topics such as Europe, the Lottery and of course their own pay, they can still produce a decent turnout. But this is rare. MPs are busier than ever doing other things, and listening to other MPs talk comes low on their list of priorities.

Tony Banks once suggested that there should be desks in the Chamber so that MPs could deal with correspondence while waiting their turn to speak. This was thought another waggish Banks joke at the time, but it might be a good idea. Members could work uninterrupted by telephones or constituents, and the standard of debate would rise as other MPs tried to make their colleagues look up and listen.

Most Ministers and their Shadows simply work their dreary way through the speech in front of them. You sometimes wonder why they even bother. Often a Minister will make a statement to the two or three dozen MPs who have bothered to stay behind after Question Time. Meanwhile, the smattering of journalists above his head will be flipping through the text in a quarter of the time it takes him to read it out loud. Why not offer the same facilities to MPs? They are busy people, too.

For many MPs, their duties in the Mother of Parliaments have shrunk to a forty-eight-hour week, running from PM's Questions on Tuesday through to the end of the same event on Thursday. It is no good blaming them. We are always being told that modern technology has made the old office redundant; why not Westminster too? Most of an MP's job can be done at home. Physically turning up at Parliament is for some a way of avoiding work, or at least

avoiding their constituents. The scandal about Annie's Bar, briefly the setting for a feeble TV situation comedy, is not that it is full of drunken MPs, but that it isn't. Most nights they are tucked up at home.

It is now rare for an important government announcement to be made in the Chamber. Everything is signalled in advance through leaks and briefs by the ever-burgeoning teams of spin doctors. (One of their new jobs is giving top-secret, deep-background briefings to journalists, and then, when the articles appear in the papers, writing furious denunciations of the reporters concerned, so as to protect themselves from the people they have abused in the briefings. It is indeed a difficult and demanding job.)

There are many reasons for the slow death of the parliamentary debate. MPs now have better equipped offices and larger staffs. Word-processors, as ever, have increased rather than reduced the amount of work which has to be done: if you don't send a long and sympathetic letter to an unfortunate constituent, your rival might.

MPs also have a live feed from the Chamber – necessary now that offices are spread up to ten minutes' walk from the House. For example, the pleasantly furnished quarters at 1 Parliament Street have television monitors, decent food, a friendly bar, and even a shop. Why cross the street? Since you don't need to be there to hear what's being said, you don't bother to go there, so fewer people speak, and there's less reason than ever to appear.

But the most important element in this spiral of decline (sorry, the clichés are catching) is broadcasting. College Green, the narrow triangle of grass opposite Victoria Tower, is now the unofficial media encampment whenever important news breaks. At one point during John Major's resignation as Tory leader – or 'cry for help memo' – I

counted twenty-three camera
crews jostling each other for a
position which would get Big
Ben in shot but exclude all the
other cameras. College Green
has become Glastonbury for the
chattering classes, and is now a
tourist attraction, like Trafalgar
Square, only with MPs instead
of pigeons. It is hard to believe,
but on one occasion I saw Mrs

Teresa Gorman set upon by a gang of admiring (female) groupies. It
seemed drug-induced, and in some ways it was: HRT versus EEC.

Back in the Commons, Labour MPs were trying to get the subject
of the Prime Minister's resignation raised as a subject for debate. But
the Deputy Speaker was firm. The House debates what is on the
Order Paper, and the world can wait. When the entire country – TV,
radio, newspapers, saloon bar, Clapham omnibus – is devoted to a
single topic, with the one exception of the Commons itself, we may
wonder for a moment what it exists for.

At less hectic times, or in poor weather, MPs and Ministers
throng number 4 Millbank, the building which houses ITN and the
BBC's vast Westminster staff. This is where most yearn to be. Sit in
the Chamber and you are heard by a few colleagues and the
minuscule minority which is watching the live feed on cable
television. Appear on local radio in your constituency, on ITN's
House of House, *The World at One*, or the big prize, *News at Ten*, and
your views are known to thousands, even millions.

There's permanent buzz there, noticeably absent from the
Chamber. When a big story is moving, astute lobby correspondents –
themselves invited in for off-the-shelf punditry – hang round the
foyer in Millbank, since MPs are more numerous there and more
accessible. None of them would dream of taking the political pulse
of the nation by sitting in the Chamber.

And in any case, TV treats politics more seriously than
Parliament. Prime Minister's Question Time deals in the cheap and
the trivial, or takes what is significant and turns it into sound bites.
TV offers lengthy discussions, hour-long analyses, and invests
politicians with the dignity they feel they deserve. To be rubbished
by Jeremy Paxman may be distressing but it brings its own prestige;
I am important enough to be abused in front of half a million people.
I matter! No one could think that while trading insults across the
House with the half dozen equally bored people on the other side.

Is the death of the Commons Chamber important? Perhaps not.
Few people pay much heed to the spoken proceedings of the
Bundestag, the Japanese Diet or the US Senate, all of which pass
laws for reasonably successful nations. Perhaps we should bid it the
same slow and regretful farewell we seem to be bestowing on our
Royal Family.

CLINTON:
Oversexed, overweight and over here

- 520·11·11·94 - ~ © Steve Bell 1994 -

More characters from the Long March of British History began the long march down the gallery. The Lord Great Chamberlain. The Gentleman Usher of the Black Rod – Robin to his Blackman.

In November President Clinton spoke to both Houses of Parliament, in the famous Royal Gallery. With its embossed wallpaper, its gleaming red and gold, its riot of gilt decorations, the place gives Americans a chance to get a sense of something they rarely see – the inside of an Indian restaurant.

The rites began long before the President's entrance. The Leader of the Opposition (John Redwood) arrived, closely followed by the Leader of the Opposition to the Opposition (Robin Cook).

Then, ablaze in a dress of royal purple, Lois Blasenheim, researcher and companion to that most ancient of traditional figures: Dennis Skinner, the Beast of Bolsover. So as well as the Queen's Beasts, we had the Beast's Queen.

More characters from the Long March of British History began the long march down the gallery. The Lord Great Chamberlain. The Gentleman Usher of the Black Rod – Robin to his Blackman. The First Secretary of State, the Deputy Prime Minister and Michael Heseltine (though since these three were all the same person, the

procession was shorter than it might have been).

A ravishing creature with long blond hair and black tights rose to welcome Mr Clinton. It was a moment of pure suspense. Would he invite this vision back to his hotel room? He did not, partly because Hillary was up on the platform, partly because it turned out to be the Lord Chancellor, in a wig.

Mr Clinton rose. In all modern Presidential speeches, the setting is used as a backdrop for the sound bites carefully prepared in advance for the evening news back home. In this task, the President is greatly helped by the White House press corps, a court as large and loyal as enjoyed by any mediaeval king. They lined the walls.

But first, he had some news for us. It appeared that the US navy was to name one of its new ships after a celebrated British Prime Minister.

We gasped. After all, warships are usually grey, wet and liable to be sunk at any moment. Surely not… No, it turned out to be the *USS Winston Churchill*.

The next day Mr Clinton travelled to Northern Ireland. An American President is thought to have almost magical powers in Ireland, representing those who managed to escape the British and prosper at the same time. Ronald Reagan once visited a village called Ballyporeen, where a man called Michael Regan, thought to be his ancestor, had lived before emigrating to America. As the President mused at the time, 'If Michael Regan had never left Ballyporeen, I wouldn't be here today.'

Mr Clinton's day was freighted with symbols, none more so than

the walkabouts. He plunged freely into crowds who were lining streets so dangerous that at the height of the Troubles you were almost half as likely to be murdered as you are today in Washington, DC.

But this was during the IRA cease-fire, and the mood was cheerful and relaxed. An old shabby Santa Claus, possibly given leave by some failing department store, stood by the side of the road. 'Would you be one of those FBI men protecting the President?' an RUC sergeant asked cheerfully. Over-excited TV commentators began to jabber. President Clinton was being protected by Ninja Turtles, they said. This sounded extreme even for an American President, but it turned out they meant the special policemen who patrol the Belfast sewers.

The President's absurd thirty-two-vehicle motorcade (in the US it can run to nearly forty limos, buses and motorbikes, sometimes actually gridlocking itself in New York's convoluted one-way system) swept up the Shankill Road, occupying much of its length. Serious cleaning-up had gone on and the street's most cherished graffito, 'Fuck the Next Pope', had disappeared.

At the Mackie factory, which straddles the peace line, he paused for some remarks about the need for peace. Such remarks, anodyne anywhere else in the world, can be controversial in Ulster. He endorsed the notion of the IRA, or at least Sinn Fein, having some role in talks, provided they had a cease-fire at the time. 'Those who renounce violence and take their own risks for peace are entitled to be full participants in the peace process.'

'Never!' shouted a voice belonging to a former DUP councillor called Cedric Wilson, a poor man's Ian Paisley. Anthony Lake, Clinton's national security adviser, looked anxious. In America nobody ever shouts 'Never!' at the President. Michael Ancram, the British number two, was on hand to reassure him. 'To get only one person shouting "Never!" in Northern Ireland is a miracle,' he said.

Shortly after his handshake with Gerry Adams on the Falls Road, the President's motorcade whisked him to a business park in the east of the city. The businessmen who operated the small units there had received American grants which had enabled them to start up, and they were there to testify to the wonders they had been enabled to perform. Each explained in painstaking detail what they had done with the money, why, and how. Each small speech was intensely, stupefyingly, majestically boring.

The President looked up. He looked down. He took many unnecessarily small sips from a mug of coffee. He pulled a pen from his pocket, and, while gazing as gravely as he could at each entrepreneur, appeared to be taking notes on what they were saying. By half-standing and craning my head, I could see that he wasn't writing anything.

The businessmen droned on. Mr Clinton seemed to be in some physical distress. His eyes bulged. His lips curled around his teeth, so that although his jaw was open his mouth was tightly closed. It was soon quite

obvious what was happening: he was corpsing, and was terrified that he would not be able to help himself and would suddenly burst, right in the middle of a disquisition on the role of tax rebates for companies with less than £500,000 turnover in a competitive environment…

Then, all of a sudden, relief arrived. One of the businessmen said, 'Wull, Mr President, yew would hardly expect to come to East Belfast without having the Gospel quoted to you!'

Mr Clinton looked alarmed. Then he realised that this was meant to be a joke. Twenty minutes of repressed and frustrated laughter surged out in one mighty bellow. He held his sides. He rocked around in his seat. He spluttered out his coffee, and his eyes narrowed tightly as if he was afraid that tears of mirth would pour out.

It was a wonderful, joyous moment, and almost made up for the fact that his pleas for peace had been – as we later learned – totally and completely ignored.

RABBITING ON AT QUESTION TIME

What we need in the Commons is a Question Time Bunny, who would offer his own running commentary on the questions and replies.

Now and again someone tries to reform Prime Minister's Question Time. Sometimes it's the Prime Minister. John Major said that he hoped MPs would give him advance notice of the topics they proposed to raise, so that he could provide thoughtful and informative answers. The first MP who did this was Mr Paul Flynn, of Newport, who was rewarded for his courtesy with a blast of party-political invective. Politicians remind me of Aesop's fable about the scorpion who begs a frog for a lift across a river. The frog demurs, worried the scorpion will sting him. The scorpion scoffs, pointing out that they would both drown. But he does sting the frog, and as they go under, he explains, 'I can't help it. It's in my nature.'

Politicians are similar. Even when they are discussing such horrors as the Dunblane massacre, you can see them trying to work out how, and when, they can make a party-political point without appearing too appallingly tasteless. The chance even to imply that the other side was in some small way responsible for that monstrosity is just too tempting. It took months, but finally there was a Party split on gun-control laws. They always get there in the end. They can't help it; it's in their nature.

Prime Minister's Questions are broadcast on TV in America where, we are often told, they are 'cult viewing'. Since the session appears on cable, and since the C-Span channel is constantly being dropped by cable companies across the US, the cult must be very small. Nevertheless I have met Americans who have watched it, and they express themselves bewildered. Betty Boothroyd, the Speaker, says she gets more complaints about it than any other single topic.

Often it resembles a nightmarish train journey. You are sitting with your paper, when suddenly a gang of football fans gets on. They are drinking Special Brew straight from the can, but while being noisy and boisterous, they do not appear hostile. You bury yourself in the paper, hoping they won't pay any heed to you. For a while they don't, then running out of stupid jokes to make, and their burping contest beginning to pall, they notice you hiding away. 'Ere, wozza marrer wiv 'im? 'Ere mate, have a drink, gow on...' Suddenly, just in the nick of time, it's 3.30 and you can clamber gratefully from the train.

This is why Mr Blair's proposed reforms will not succeed either. He envisages a single half-hour period each week. Instead of cheap political cracks and bootlicking from the government side, there will be a constructive discussion of the great issues facing the nation, thus:

Tory MP: 'Will the Prime Minister be kind enough to share with us his thoughts on the economy?'

The Prime Minister (Mr Blair): 'With great pleasure. I am delighted to report an encouraging decrease in unemployment and a heartening estimate from the Treasury that we shall have growth of 2.9 per cent this year. But I must enter a small caveat. Honourable Members know that these predictions can resemble weather forecasts – they are not invariably accurate! [Laughter.] Inflation remains steady, I am pleased to say, but I for one am not entirely sanguine about an early cut in interest rates.'

'However, the situation overall is reasonably good, and I am happy to take this opportunity to thank the Loyal Opposition for all the spadework they did while in government. Their admirably prudent policies may, somewhat unjustly, have cost them the last election. But they laid a sure foundation for us to build on, and I am certain their vote of thanks will come from the judgement of history.'

The Leader of the Opposition (Mr Redwood): 'I thank the right honourable gentleman for those gracious remarks. While we were naturally regretful at losing the last election, I am sure I speak for my colleagues on these benches when I say that we could not have entrusted our country to safer hands than his...'

Of course it wouldn't work out like that. It would descend quickly to the usual frantic bickering. Like the Americans, we now have the permanent election campaign in this country, a campaign which begins the day the results are announced, and continues without cease to the next poll. In the permanent campaign, every single speech is a party-political broadcast, every single line uttered in the Chamber must make its contribution to the river of propaganda.

For this reason, the session often has the air of a tea-time in the lounge of an old folks' home. Everyone is talking, but no one is listening to anybody else. It becomes a series of separate monologues, ignored by everyone except the Speaker. Greasers grease, purely in order to be heard by the Whips. Opposition MPs produce their own carefully honed and market-tested phrases, also handed to them on convenient pieces of paper. Those with sound bites to utter, utter them. Nothing relates to anything else. Topics are raised not to be discussed, merely as an excuse to change the subject. ('I am surprised that on a day when British troops have come under fire in Bosnia, you choose to raise the topic of unemployment...')

Prime Minister's Questions were never faced by Gladstone or Churchill. But then they didn't have permanent campaigns. In those days you governed the country for four years or so, then stirred your stumps and made a few speeches, which were reported respectfully and at some length. Mr Attlee used to have his wife drive him to election meetings, and on their way they would eat sandwiches by the roadside. Attlee was so ignorant about public relations that when his Press Association printer – which he used exclusively to follow the cricket scores – began to tap out the contents of a briefing by his Press Secretary, he asked why there was an account of the Cabinet meeting 'on my cricket machine'.

Macmillan was the first Prime Minister to have a Question Time all to himself, and in those days the questions were sometimes genuine requests for information. This was appropriate since Macmillan was probably the first Prime Minister to understand the importance of the sound bite: the 'wind of change'; 'most of our people have never had it so good'. Even in the days before broadcasting, Harold Wilson knew how to use Prime Minister's Questions as a gladiatorial tourney. His intention was to depict Sir Alec Douglas-Home as elderly, out of touch, out of date, closer to the grouse moor than to ordinary British people, and this he did by tormenting him twice a week. This heartened his own backbenchers, and word percolated through to the public through press reports.

Margaret Thatcher regarded the session as her 'hotline' to the British people and would spend hours preparing over a sandwich lunch, obsessively going over every possible reponse to every possible topic.

Now, with the Chamber on television, PMQs have become an integral part of the permanent campaign. Mr Blair invariably has a sound bite ready. This is constantly mocked by Mr Major. 'Well, it took rather a long time to get to the sound bite, and I don't think it was worth waiting for!' he will say, but that remark is never broadcast, while the sound bite usually is. Mr Blair knows how to give the TV people a 'clean feed'. He will begin by saying something like, 'Doesn't it prove once again that this government...' His words may be drowned by the baying opposite, but he will always start again, even if he needs the Speaker to help him obtain silence. The result is a crisp few seconds on the evening news. Since the

British Politics Explained No: 452 *in a series of* 309
PRIME MINISTER'S QUESTION TIME
— OR —
WHICH PINHEAD CAN ACCOMMODATE THE MOST ANGELS

- 721 · 1.2.'96 -

© Steve Bell 1996

published by the KEEP IT LOW KEEP IT FILTHY CAMPAIGN *in the interests of a cleaner political environment.*

broadcasters are obliged to demonstrate impartiality, they more or less have to use the sound bite as spoken. Whether Blair 'won' or 'lost' the exchanges is beside the point – his two dozen words have won their millions of listeners.

There are many real ways in which PMQs could be improved. My own idea came to me after I had watched the News Bunny, the creation of L!ve TV's Kelvin MacKenzie. At home of an evening I like to catch *Topless Darts at Eleven*. This is not, of course, because I like to see semi-nude young women engaged in activities which cause their various body parts to move independently. For one thing, the participants are only rarely good looking, and some look distressingly as if their silicone implants have just leaked out. My fellow feeling is with the presenter who, like me, earns his daily living by commenting on an absurd and degrading spectacle. (Like me, he goes in for heavy sarcasm. 'And now the crowds are stampeding to catch a glimpse of Vanna and Kimberly,' while the camera shows an old man snoozing in a deckchair.)

Then the News Bunny appears. He is a human-sized rabbit with a mocking smile and cute whiskers. He stands behind the newsreader, who cannot see him, which is fortunate, since he or she must keep a reasonably straight face. The News Bunny offers a mimed gloss on the various stories – joy if a British team wins some sporting event, sorrow if a child's death is reported, glee when Princess Diana attends a gala preview.

What we need in the Commons is a Question Time Bunny, who

would offer his own running commentary on the questions and replies. For example, when a notorious greaser such as Charles Goodson-Wickes rises to say, 'The vast majority of my constituents agree about the need to increase lenient sentences. Is it not another example of hypocrisy that the Opposition voted against this,' the Question Time Bunny would bend down and stick out its tongue to lick an imaginary boot, or worse.

Then when the Prime Minister asserted that under his government, crime had fallen for the first time in forty years, the Bunny would have expressed comical, eye-rolling incredulity, since overall crime has doubled since 1979.

The Bunny would be quite impartial. If Mr Major landed a blow on the Opposition (for example, with a favourite trick – making some apparently impeccable right-wing remark then revealing that he had been quoting a Labour front-bencher), the furry fellow would alternately clutch his sides and wave an admonitory finger at the Opposition.

He would be on the lookout for Majorisms. For instance, the Prime Minister often kicks into somewhat camp mode when he is assailing Mr Ashdown, the Liberal leader. 'There's no point in you living in some Disneyland, waving your arms around,' he once shouted at Mr Ashdown, while still, somehow, on the subject of crime. The Bunny would do a mincing walk and make limp-wristed gestures with his paws.

He would be particularly harsh on what passes for humour among MPs. Sir Patrick Cormack tried to make a joke about the Liberals: 'Will you give a firm undertaking that you will not take advice on law and order from a Party that would change the meaning of the "Sunday joint"?' the Question Time Bunny would roll over and play dead, its little paws quivering in the air.

SEND IN THE COWS!!

'I eat beef, my wife eats beef, our two sons and one daughter eat beef, and our six grandchildren eat beef!' said Nicholas Winterton. So if his family are all suddenly wiped out, like the dinosaurs, we shall know the reason why.

Back in the dawn of time, towards the end of the last Labour government, Ministers had drafted new regulations concerning what could go into cattle feed. When Mrs Thatcher came to power in 1979, these were quietly dropped, and all sorts of disgusting stuff went into animals who were later digested by us: mashed-up sheep's brains, for instance, and chicken manure, which is supposed to be rich in protein, though why we should want to eat the stuff which the chicken is anxious to extrude, I do not know.

Ten years later, in 1989, the Labour front-bench spokesman Ron Davies predicted that the relaxed regulations could lead to disease being passed on down the food chain to humans. His warning was scoffed at by the government and ignored. In fact Mr Davies is used to being

179

WELCOME TO GREAT BRITAIN

ignored; being Old Labour and so mistrusted by Tony Blair, he is in the unique position of a front-bench spokesman to whom nobody listens.

So the first full-blown mad cow scare came in 1990. The threat to the huge British beef industry was obvious, and Ministers moved immediately to calm public fears. John Gummer, then the Minister of Agriculture, was photographed feeding a beefburger to his daughter Cordelia. Curiously, this image had the opposite effect to the one intended. It seemed to imply that Mr Gummer had some doubts about the safety of the burger, and was trying it out on his daughter, just in case.

Then matters went quiet until March 1996, when scientists decided that it might conceivably be possible to contract the disease CJD by eating beef from cows infected with BSE. The news leaked out, and to be fair to the government, they decided to level with Parliament. The Health Secretary, Stephen Dorrell, was dispatched to the House to bring us the bad news. Mr Dorrell was solid. 'We must not overreact,' he said and then, in riotously judicious fashion added, 'just as we must not under-react.' In contrast to Mr Gummer, he offered no photo opportunities, and even declined to say whether he would give beef to his own children. 'This is not a time for a lay Minister to offer his views,' he said. It actually translates into English as 'I'm not going to say anything which might get me in more trouble later, and I'm certainly not going to react like that prancing prat, Gummer.'

O THE ROAST BEEF OF OLD ENGLAND, &c.

In spite of Mr Dorrell's caution, it was clear that the government was facing serious difficulties. As always it was necessary to find a scapegoat. The usual choice on these occasions is the Labour Party, which can always be blamed for seventeen years of misrule. The fact that they have been in Opposition throughout that period is seen as a feeble excuse.

The scapegoat took human shape in the form of Harriet Harman, then the Shadow Health Secretary. She had a difficult task. She did not want to start a massive health scare, but on the other hand, she did. Or at least start an anti-government scare. 'Today in the House, the Minister has, I am sure inadvertently, given out more false reassurance. The Chief Medical Officer says he will continue to eat beef. Would he feed it to his grandchildren? If we don't have full information and full exposure, the public's reaction will be one of fear.'

By this time the Tories were enraged. Their normal method of expressing disapproval does sound much like a demented mooing. 'Disgraceful!' someone shouted.

Mr Nicholas Winterton spoke for many Tories on the opening day. 'I eat beef, my wife eats beef, our two sons and one daughter eat beef, and our six grandchildren eat beef!' he said. So if the Winterton family are all suddenly wiped out, like the dinosaurs, we shall know the reason why.

Then the European Union banned the export of all British beef to anywhere in the world, and the government panicked. It became

'VERY WELL, ALONE'

even more urgent to blame the Labour Party for the crisis, and the fact that they had warned of it years ago was typical of the weasely way they had tried to wriggle out of their responsibility. Mr Dorrell was back, to accuse Labour MPs of 'the worst kind of scare-mongering – ferreting around in the sewer of political advantage'. He added petulantly that it was 'no good saying that it is unnatural for one species to eat the remains of another; that is what the meat industry is all about'.

No, it isn't. The objection to feeding cattle on animal protein is that they are vegetarians by nature and constitution. You might just as well feed your childen hay.

Mr Major also blamed the Opposition. 'Those who have destroyed confidence will be the people to blame! They sit there, and there, and there!'

Back-benchers leapt to his support. Mr David Ashby, who unsuccessfully sued the *Sunday Times* for calling him a homosexual, and who was consequently fired by his constituency, decided to go on bravely brown-nosing to the very end. BSE was not a party-political crisis, but a crisis for the whole nation. The Labour Party should stop making cheap political points.

This expressed the core Conservative position. While it was quite all right for the Opposition to criticise minor mistakes, when the government had brought us a global catastrophe, it was their job to roll up their sleeves and help pull it out of the mire.

The message from Ministers at this point was that eating beef was

STEADY AS SHE GOES

© Steve Bell 1996

751·27·3·96

perfectly safe, whatever the scheming Continentals might claim. John Major implied a new slogan: 'Eat British beef – you probably won't die.' Everyone agreed with him, or almost everybody – most of the Cabinet, many Tory back-benchers, several scientists. Against them, at this stage, were ranged nobody but a handful of malcontents, such as every other country in the world.

Mr Dorrell was so cross that at one point he said it was the public who had gone mad, rather than the cows, so making the most basic mistake in political life – blaming the voters. By this time it was clear that the Cabinet was taking leave of its collective senses. It might be time for a humane cull. A last meal of *boeuf wellington*, perhaps, swilled down with a decent botle of claret, then the stun gun in the back of the neck, and into a power-station furnace. Mr Dorrell, say, could fuel a town the size of Melton Mowbray for ten minutes. Mr Hague could power Little Rissington for a few seconds.

Meanwhile, people were beginning to feel sorry for the cows, first fed disgusting, shit-filled food, then told they had to die. (Or not told. No doubt they will one day have their own cable channel, like every other minority. 'This just in. We're all going to die! Die, I tell you! Stay with us for *Moosnight*.')

In April, Mr Hogg, who had spent several weeks shuttling among all those plump European Ministers with their wearisome sense of moral rectitude, finally lost it. He went off his bike, out of his pram, and began swinging from imaginary chandeliers. He began to rave in the House. It would be tempting to blame all that beef he is

obliged to force down his throat, those pounds of fillet, sirloin, topside, steak-and-kidney pies, hamburgers and corned-beef hash he is obliged to cram in. He was by then the only Tory MP from whom the phrase 'Fancy a nice bit of skirt?' would evince only groans.

He left yet another meeting at 6.00 in the morning, gave a press conference lasting twenty-two seconds, then jammed on his ridiculous wide-brim hat, which comes from some hinterland between metropolitan London and the rich cattle lands of the Argentinian pampas. He is a gaucho from the Groucho.

His speech became stippled and staccato. Exclamation marks appeared in the most unlikely places. 'There are encouraging! signs that! confidence is! returning. Retailers say their! customers are! looking for beef again. So! those with! cattle to send to market should know there! are buyers for British beef.'

When his opposite number, Gavin Strang, asked how many cattle would have to be slaughtered, and when the ban on British beef might be lifted, Mr Hogg finally departed from his trolley, and went mad before our eyes.

He started slowly and menacingly, like a TV barrister who has suddenly come upon the crucial evidence. ('Begging yer pardon, sir, but I found this letter in the lodger's jacket. D'yer think it might be important?' 'Mrs Hodgkinson, this letter might! just save! a man's life!')

'Let me first make this point,' he said. Then he got louder. 'So that the House can hear! it! very! clearly! The honourable gentleman did

184

NOT condemn the ban. He has expressed his *understanding* of the ban! Those [*drop to sneery voice*] who have heard you will take! COMFORT!' Mere typography cannot do justice to the controlled hysteria, the dampened dementia. The Opposition roared with glee. The moment they had awaited for two weeks had finally arrived.

Nearly two months later we declared war on Europe. The Prime Minister announced his policy of non-cooperation to a sombre Commons Chamber: 'I have to tell the House that I regard such action as wilful disregard of Britain's interests… I have to tell the House, that without progress towards the lifting of the ban, we cannot be expected to continue to cooperate on other Community business.'

No doubt he was deliberately making us hear the echoes of another address to the nation, almost fifty-seven years before: 'I have to tell you that no such undertaking has been received.' We almost expected to hear the first air-raid sirens, and a lone Messerschmitt to be seen wheeling over Lowestoft.

But this too was the phoney war. It ended the following month, when John Major, having been forced to accept damaging and humiliating terms, came back to the Commons to declare victory and to abuse roundly anyone who disagreed with him.

Mr Major's ability to drag a public-relations stunt out of the jaws of defeat is unparalleled. Employed by the Germans to put the best gloss on the 1914 Armistice, he would have explained how 'four years of brave and resolute resistance have enabled us to agree with

185

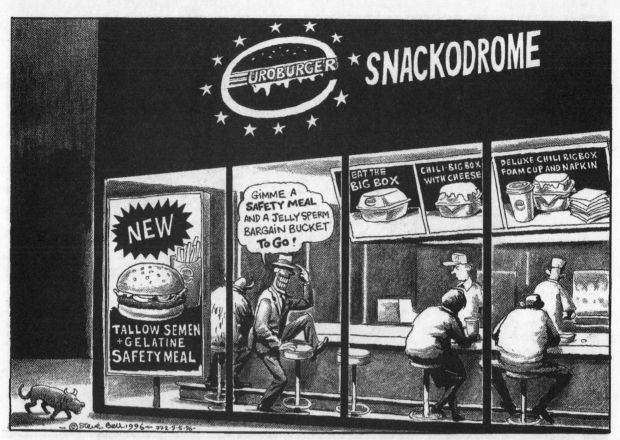

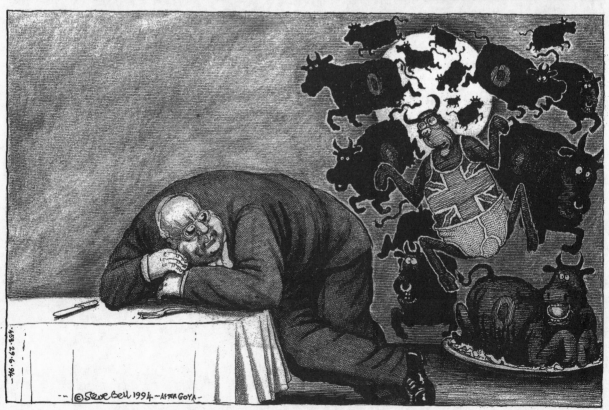

our European partners a satisfactory framework agreement on which we can now build'.

As spokesman for Dr Crippen: 'My client enjoyed a fine sea cruise with his delightful companion, Miss Ethel Le Neve. It is a breathtaking misunderstanding of the situation to claim that, as a result of the subsequent court case, Dr Crippen is to be "executed". He would certainly have died in the long term, and the court's decision merely reflects an ongoing accelerated demise programme.'

The phrase 'accelerated programme', referring to the sixty-five thousand cows who, it was agreed with the Europeans, are now to be slaughtered sooner rather than later, has a chilling ring to it. There are those who fear that one day it will be adapted as a pilot scheme for the long-term care of elderly British humans. After all, like the cows, they are going to die sooner or later.

MAN SUCCESSFULLY
NEGOTIATING COWPAT

—AFTER MICHELANGELO'S SLAVES
(FLORENCE, ACCADEMIA)

NEWS FROM NOWHERE

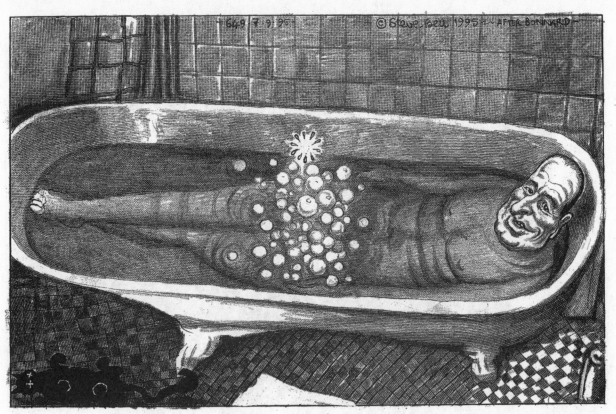